Scandals, Scoundrels, Deception, and Depravity

Genesis and the Sovereign

David W. Hall

The Covenant Foundation
Powder Springs, GA

© 2022
The Covenant Foundation
648 Goldenwood Court
Powder Springs, GA 30127
(david.hall@midwaypca.org)

All Rights reserved. No part of this publication may be reproduced or transmitted in any form or by any means, electronic or mechanical, without written permission from the publisher, except for inclusion in a magazine, newspaper, or broadcast.

Hall, David W.
Scandals, Scoundrels, Deception, and Depravity

1. Genesis; 2. Biblical Studies;
3. Old Testament Commentary

Printed in the United States of America

Table of Contents

Preface	5
1. Abraham's First Deception: Wife-Trafficking	8
2. Abraham's Military Industrial Complex and Melchizedek	15
3. The Wrong Way to Build a Covenant Family	24
4. Doubt and Miracle—Abraham and Sarah Laughing	31
5. Abraham, The Negotiator	35
6. Loving the City: Sodom Does Not End up Gay	41
7. Routine Ruses, Embarrassing Excuses	47
8. Fear and Trembling	51
9. How I Met Your Mother	56
10. The End of an Era: The Continuation of Some Things	61
11. Wife-Deceit: Third Strike and You're Out	65
12. The Deceiver Grasps	68
13. The Deceiver/Conniver Realizes his Need for God	72
14. The Conniver Out-Connived	77
15. The Out-Conniver Out-Connived	81
16. Focus OFF the Family	85
17. The Out-Conniver Returns to Face his Past	88
18. The Scandalous Rape of a Sister: A Thousand Eyes For One Eye	90
19. On Family Genealogies	93
20. A Brat and his Brother's Deception	97
21. A Strong Female Gets Justice	101
22. #NotTrue	105
23. From Prison Back to the Palace	109
24. Economics and Politics During a Famine: Sovereignty In Action	113

25. Joseph's Pranking; Joseph's Provision	120
26. Providence Continued	123
27. No Longer Concealed: God's Purpose Now Revealed	126
28. A Family Reunion and Resettlement	128
29. Preparing for Famine . . . and Exodus	131
30. Providence Through and Through	134
31. Blessings and AntiBlessings	137
32. The End of the Beginning	141
33. Where did all this come from?	144
Appendix A: Genesis in the Gospels	159
Appendix B: Genesis According to the Apostles	160

Preface

While teaching a Bible study recently, several themes leapt out of the pages of a biblical book that I have studied often. The middle and latter parts of the Book of Genesis present portrayals of families and heroes who are as flawed as . . . alas, we are. As such this provides a striking proof (over and over again) that the biblical record, properly grasped, is neither glossy mythology nor hagiolatry.

Instead, it is the truthful and historical record, selected by an editor to be sure, to teach enduring truths. Of course, that editor was God himself (2 Tim. 3:16).

Not only do we see that these narratives are reliable and true, but they also present family deception, self-deception, and scandal in the earliest periods of human history.

Nihil Novi Sub Sole

The value of viewing more history instead of less leads us to ask two important questions: Do the dynamics of human interaction and relationships change over time? How does this affect applicability of a knowledge-base over two thousand years old? Our answer, although admitting many technological fluxes, is to side with Solomon: *nihil novi sub sole* (Eccl. 1:9). Indeed, in terms of human dynamics there is little new under the sun—except the technologies that are harnessed in the pursuit of cultural ends. Most of the strengths of society, as well as its errors, have already been tried or discovered. It is important to know from the outset that human dynamics are largely unchanged over time. Thus, the Bible is still relevant to social and interpersonal matters.

In mature reflection on human culture, history is a stalwart assistant as a corroborating guide. One assumption is that over even large periods of time, the human condition and social solutions are basically constant. Therefore, it is believed that one is unwise to fail to benefit from what has successfully worked in other eras.

Strikingly similar ethical, social, and environmental dynamics were present early on in the OT. Thus, our situations are not really novel. Though sobering to realize that in many respects the problems and foundational dynamics have barely changed over time, the course of wisdom requires us to be reticent to endorse social proposals that begin by defining the challenges as totally unique, non-normal, or without parallel. To esteem our own exigencies as categorically unique or a 'crisis,' is either a by-product of inordinate fear or *hubris*, which leads to a skewed perspective that tends to diminish rational solutions in deference to the perceived magnitude of the 'crisis.' By the time of Abraham (ca. 2000 BC), the following socio-political dynamics were already present:

- difficulty of labor to provide necessities for living (Gen. 3:18-19)
- fratricide (Gen. 4:8)
- violent homicide (Gen. 4:23)
- moral wickedness (Gen. 6:5 and 8:20)
- ecological disaster (Gen. 7-9)
- sexual sin (Gen. 9:22)
- tribal (gang?) warfare (Gen. 10:8-9)
- infertility (Sarah)
- competition for income (Gen. 13:8-9)
- consequences stemming from military conquests (Gen. 14)
- ethnic hostility (Gen. 16:12)
- homosexuality (Gen. 19:5)
- family alienation (Gen. 21:8 ff.)

Thus, with what sounds like the findings of causes of societal ill from a modern Commission, we will want to be careful before pronouncing that we are in a completely new or unique situation. Such claims will have to be scrutinized and judged by the principle enunciated by Solomon that, "There is nothing new under the sun" (Eccl. 1:9-11; 3:15).[1] That being the case, the plethora of problems takes

---

[1] Thomas Sowell, *The Vision of the Anointed* (New York: Basic Books, 1995), 6-9 provides an excellent aetiology of modern failures to remedy manufactured crises.

on a different cast than when one is led to believe that solutions must be created *de novo*. If the problems and dynamics of the human *polis* are largely static, then we are afforded a calmer opportunity to assess solutions with more reason and balance than if we are impetuously required to create a state without the larger principles given by the great Creator of society. One of the aspects of this commentary is that both problems and solutions will be normatively similar over time. Certainly, there is external change in societies, but that is not to say that the root problems or remedial reforms have changed substantially. Once again, an aged set of norms may be more helpful than the latest studies, particularly if such modernity-biased studies are flawed at the outset with an ignorance of historical similarities.

This small collection explores those and seeks to tie them together as a unity. This great literature—inspired for sure—is also very instructive to teach modern people how to live, especially how *not* to deal with one another, and something of the long effects of sinful behavior.

As many times as I've taught through these narratives, they are not only evergreen but they also address, if we have ears to hear, some of the thorniest issues of our lives today.

Note: I do not explore the history presented in Genesis 1-11 to avoid controversy. To the contrary, I've actually written and published a good bit on the historic view of creation.[2] So this present author is hardly deficient in commenting on those passages and continues to believe that all the other, very creative and innovative theories will be judged by history to have been fabricated attempts to mold the Bible to some science or theory of the day. Not wanting to do that with protology (the study of origins), neither do I wish to distort the teachings of Gen. 12-50 into myths, frameworks, hero tales that did not happen, nor anything else other than true history with massive application.

So while we may not (with Julie Andrews' character in the *Sound of Music*) "start at the very beginning," we may return to it often.

---

[2] See David Hagopian, ed., *The Genesis Debate* (Crux Press, 2000); David W. Hall and Joseph A. Pipa, eds., *Did God Create in Six Days?* (Tolle Lege Press, 2006); and my *Holding Fast to Creation* (2011).

Abram's First Deception: Wife Trafficking (Genesis 12:10-20)

Abraham is a giant of faith. Few will ever come close either to his deserved stature or to his faith. He was a friend of God.

When we are first introduced to him, we see his faith primarily as prompt, unflinching obedience. Terah (Abram's father) had three sons: Abram, Nahor, and Haran (11:27). That third son, Haran, was Lot's father, and Haran died before the family migrated away from Ur (Babylon) for Canaan. Abram and Nahor, the surviving sons of Terah, along with their wives and children, set out with Terah for Canaan. Abram's wife, Sarai, was unable to bear children (11:30).

This extended family set out for Canaan but settles 600 miles northwest in the region of Haran. Terah, Abram's father, lived a full life and passed away in Haran, not making it to the land of Canaan. That would be left up to Abram.

Genesis 12 informs us how this giant of the faith, responded to God's call. God called him to leave behind his country, and his father's house to settle where the Lord led. Abram obeyed and left behind the things that are most comforting to most of us: family, friends, locale, business, and familiarity.

God promised to bless Abram and turn his small beginnings into a great nation. Abram's reputation would also be great, and all people would be blessed through him. Not limiting these promises merely to one ethnic group, God destined Abram to be a blessing to the entire world, and that would come through the seed of Abraham, Jesus (See Galatians 3:6-9 for more on this).

So, Abram obeyed and left his comforts to follow God. In doing so, he was a missionary (leaving his own culture to serve God in another), a blessing to humanity, and would become the head of a covenant. Abram was 75 (12:4) when he left, and he traveled another 275 miles south from Haran to Canaan. Of course, he took his wife and his nephew Lot and all his possessions. Apparently, Abram had prospered in Haran, and his estate was growing. It would soon become a huge business/army/family.

When Abram reached Canaan, the Lord settled him there and promised that his offspring would receive this territorial tract. And Abram responded to God by building an altar of remembrance there (12:7). As was his habit, whenever he progressed and had a significant spiritual milestone, he built an altar (12:8; 13:18) to honor the Lord's blessing. These altars were markers for others, as well as for his own family, to recollect how God had worked in their lives.

Abram was truly a giant in the faith.

However, respecting such peak performance, was he a perfect saint? Should we follow him in all that he did? Or should we not value his faith, while simultaneously recognizing his imperfections?

The balance of Genesis 12 is sobering and should be included in the resume of Abram. It seems that God, at least, wanted this part included.

Briefly, let me ask three questions of the latter half of Genesis 12: (1) What did Abram do?; (2) Why is this included?; and (3) How should we view our spiritual grandparents?

What did Abram do?

A famine occurred in Canaan (later God will use the same catastrophe to preserve Joseph and his family), and Abram did what most fathers/husbands would do. There were no grocery stores, Amazon food delivery, or Instacart services in that day. He had to go and find food for a growing family. So, he went to Egypt, which was the most powerful and plentiful nation of the day.

The form of government in Egypt at the time (the Pharaoh was likely Khofu) was a Monarchy Plus. By that I mean, there were no democracies, no republics, no parliaments—only a sole sovereign, whose power was unchecked. Moreover, this was Monarchy Plus, since Pharaoh was also viewed as divine. Suffice it to say that such a Monarch is to be feared and not trifled with.

Just prior to crossing over the border into Egypt, Abram thought up a scheme that might be thought of as wife-trafficking today. Recognizing that Sarai was beautiful (12:11; note, at age 65, she was likely comparable to a woman half that age in view of the lifespans at the time) and that she was at the top of her game—very attractive—Abram knew that he could be killed summarily in order for anyone to take gorgeous Sarai as a wife. Any Egyptian or Pharaoh himself, could quickly calculate that the shortest distance between point "A" (Sarai) and point "B" (taking Sarai as a wife) was to eliminate Abram.

Thus, Abram concocted a story that you might not want to try at home. He sold Sarai on the proposition that when they entered Egypt, she should claim to be his sister "so that I will be treated well for your sake and my life will be spared because of you." (12:13) This was clearly deceitful, and it was not exactly loving and protecting of his wife. To be sure, times were rough, but this hardly seems to justify wife-trafficking.

What Abram did, then was to enter Egyptian territory, and when Pharaoh's officials took note of her beauty. They reported it, and she was taken into his palace (12:15) as part of his household—a marriage. And Pharaoh treated Abram, thought to be Sarai's brother, well, and Abram's business and holdings grew dramatically.

While Abram's net worth is increasing, however, God brought a pandemic onto Pharaoh and his household because of the unrecognized impropriety of Abram's bargain. Sarai had no rights, no legal standing to refuse Pharaoh anything, and we don't know the exact length of time of this arrangement. Nevertheless, God brought a severe, incurable disease on the land, beginning at Pharaoh's palace, and he quickly rooted out the cause of this divine judgment: it was Abram's deceit. Note, that even this Pharaoh seemed to believe that God existed, could intervene in history, and that he judged immorality

When Pharaoh learned all this, he summoned Abram and confronted him (12:18), asking why he deceived him, leading him to believe that Sarai was his sister.[3] Pharaoh said that he took her as his wife (a phrase that is not easily explained away by allegories or other rationalizations) without any knowledge or intent to commit adultery. Pharaoh quickly gives Sarai back to Abram and send him out of the country under military escort (12:20).

Presumably, the plague stopped, as the Lord protected Sarai and Pharaoh by his divine intervention. And Abram returns with his family to the land of Canaan, having become very wealthy in livestock and commodities (13:2).

Father Abram nearly sacrificed Mother Sarai, except that the Lord intervened by a plague to halt an unbeliever from any more catastrophe.

But surely, we would all advise: Don't do this! And surely, Abram would learn his lesson and never do this again—until chapter 20, where he repeats this!

Why is this included?

God, the Divine editor of Scripture, of course, could have omitted this from the record. He did not have to include Abram's deceit, cowardice, and near-disaster. Yet the Lord did not erase this episode, which is part of "all scripture" that is profitable for us (2 Tim. 3:16). To answer the question as to "why is this narrative included?" is to lead to a larger point below. But, first, let me suggest that this near-disaster is included by God purposefully to remind us that even our spiritual heroes are imperfect. Even one as great and as worthy of admiration as Abram had feet of clay and exhibits imperfections several times.

I draw two important lessons from this inclusion. *First*, God wants us to reserve our worship only for One who is truly, totally, and

---

[3] Some scholars have noted that it was a custom in the Haran region, where Abram sojourned previously, to "adopt" a wife as a sister legally for inheritance purposes and other protections. However, it is clear from both the reactions of Pharaoh and the rapid exit of Abram, that this was an act of deceit and not justified. Others note that Sarai was a relative of Abram as a possible justification for his act. Any of these could have been true, but such should not lessen Abram's culpability in this ruse. God never corrects Pharaoh for his correction of Abram. It is better for us to see these characters as they are instead of glossing over infirmities.

invincibly perfect (Heb. 7:16). Jesus Christ is the only one who has never sinned, and, while we may wish to reserve honor for those who deserve honor, our utmost respect should be reserved for Christ alone. *Second*, while we should honor those who came before us—if deserving honor—we should not view them unrealistically or as if they had no moral blemishes. All our predecessors had such, and we should guard against hagiolatry—the worship of saints. Surely, at an early stage, God included this realistic account of Abram, complete with warts and all (as Cromwell requested for his own portrait), to remind later readers that even our heroes were imperfect.

How should we view our spiritual grandparents?

So how should we view our spiritual grandparents, like Abram or any other from previous generations? We should be thankful for their example. The Book of Hebrews extols the faith of Abram and does not call on us to look down on him. His faith was exemplary.[4] We should be able to recognize true faith, and not let lapses of faith require us to dismiss our spiritual grandparents. Why, we may find out that not only did they have blind spots and lapses . . . but so do we.

It would surely be wrong and incorrect to cast Abram away because of this act—which I have to say is about as bad as it gets. But we also might want to shoulder just a little less moral superiority, acting as if we'd never have lapses of faith or make Faustian bargains. It is tempting in our day to disregard any who've gone before us who had any imperfection whatsoever. While one may do that, he will soon find out that there are no heroes or heroines; also, none of us live up to that standard of unblemished, moral perfection.

In sum, it seems that two phrases may summarize how we view our spiritual grandparents: realistically and respectfully. We should not plaster a veneer over their moral culpabilities. Our predecessors were flawed human beings, we should be realistic. However, some of them also did some things that should be respected and imitated.

---

[4] For more on this, see my short book, *Ancient Faith, Enduring Belief* (2019).

Abram was one of those. He was faithfully obedient, the first missionary, the covenant father—and yet, he did several things that we cannot commend. Of him, we should test all things and hold to that which is good (1 Thess. 5:21).

Moreover, the New Testament instructs us on how to view him. Writing to the Corinthian church in ca 55 AD, the apostle Paul tells them that all things which are contained in the previously written scriptures are exhibited for our instruction (1 Cor 10:6-11). All of the OT saints and OT episodes are included by God's divine wisdom to teach us and to serve as examples. Accordingly, God holds up strong role models, but if viewed with due realism, these are also people who were flawed but that still can be honored.

Finding that blend is often challenging. But the pursuit of correct assessment of those who have gone before us seems worth the effort.

****

For Shakespeare, "The past is prologue." The past is actually an excellent introduction to many current issues. Regrettably, however, many Christians stand upon the stage of history with virtually no idea of what has preceded. Besides being placed at a distinct disadvantage with such tardy stage entrance, Christians are finding that forsaking the best of prior thought is an extremely imprudent *modus operandi*. The seduction of the superiority of modernity blindfolds many to the past.

Many act as though their chief desire is to run away from their spiritual predecessors as far and as fast as possible. Not only do many people forsake their spiritual parents, but some contemporaries also seem to suffer from repressed memories—a dubious syndrome that allows children to slander their parents *ex post facto;* all the while, such vilification denies these deceased ancestors the opportunity to speak for themselves. If they could speak, maybe Christians would find that their spiritual parents were not as barbaric as once suspected.

I hope that the next generation will be wiser in its admiration of history than recent generations have been. Specifically, I hope that future Christians will embrace the good from their spiritual forebears rather than despise it before they even become acquainted with it. When the apostle Paul spoke of "forgetting those things which lie behind," he certainly was not advocating that Christians should become mindless about the past; yet, that is all too often the case.

Perhaps as in the words of Woody Allen: "History has to repeat itself. For no one listens the first time." Another way to see this collection of short essays is to view it as an attempt to vindicate—to vindicate some exemplary Christians who may have known and lived in far more conformity to God's will than many of us ever will. If they are our betters—despite massive maligning by modern skepticism—then it may be time to rehabilitate their reputations. Abram was surely one of these from whom we can learn.

It is also a bit comforting to realize—when we are far from perfect—that God's greatest leaders were weak in areas as well. Wisdom benefits from their good example, while ascribing true perfection to One alone.

Abraham's Military Industrial Complex and Melchizedek (Genesis 14)

Many children learn about Abraham from the Bible School song, *Father Abraham*. As such, he becomes cherubicized. Just as angels of the Bible have been turned into chubby little cherubs (instead of warriors, which is the predominant function of angels), so Abraham is frequently rendered an avuncular, harmless old man who had many sons—"And I am one of them, and so are you" repeats the universalistic jingle.

But we should not lose sight of Abraham as a man's man. He was bold, brave, adventuresome, and yes, he cut a few corners—hardly angelic but certainly worthy of imitation for his finer points.

Abram started with very little (Hebrews 11; Acts 7) but the Lord blessed him and multiplied him into a strong nation, with Abram raising up a large private army in addition to all his descendants and property.

After the near-catastrophe in Genesis 12, Abram and Lot move northward from Egypt toward Canaan. They both had significantly increased the value of their holdings and enterprise in Egypt. As a result, both Abram and Lot had many herds, possessions, and hard metals (13:2, 5). As such, they also needed quite a bit of support for their herds and flocks.

Their associates began to fight over land and resources (13:7), so Abram, the one with seniority, did something highly unusual and gracious. He realized that the two large families needed to separate, and he let the younger, Lot, choose which tract for the future. Lot observed the fertility of the Jordanian plan and claimed that territory—which is noted to be close to Sodom and Gomorrah. Even at this early stage,

Sodom was known for its rampant wickedness (13:13), but Lot made his choice for residence based on what would be best for his business, instead of considering the ill-effect of immorality. This would become important later, but for now simply note the graciousness of Abram to allow Lot to choose, the poor choice of Lot, and the Lord's blessing of Abram (13:16-17).

The Sophistication of the World in 2,000 BC

It is a temptation of the time to act as though we and our cultures are so vastly superior that, in contrast, all earlier cultures were hopelessly inferior. Reading carefully between the lines of Genesis 14 disputes that. To be sure, we have technology at our fingertips, quasi-omniscient map functions via GPS, and social media to such a degree that it may be gluttonous. Our tools are different certainly.

However, the details of chapter 14 of Genesis show us that the more things change, the more they stay the same. We find the presence of domination in these pages. One ruler, hundreds of miles away has enslaved other city-states. Taxation was so oppressive as to inspire rebellion. Slavery was real, distant governmental control was common, and weapons and warfare were sophisticated. Treaties were adopted and were customary. Moreover, the power of confederacies was known at this early stage of human organization.

In this case, a Western Confederation, consisting of five city-states, had allied against the most powerful leader of the day. Those five nations, located near modern day Palestine were each led by a king. These civic entities had far outgrown a mere tribal or family governance. Each of these cities—Sodom, Gomorrah, Admah, Zeboiim, and Bela—were large enough to sport their own government, led by a king.

The Eastern Confederation similarly had kings at the head of their government, and that alliance consisted of Elam (Kederlaomer), Goiim (Tidal), Shinar (Amraphel), and Ellasar (Arioch). Interestingly, the four-nation Eastern Confederacy is clearly the more dominant, led by Kederlaomer. Another indication of his prowess is seen in Genesis chapter 14, which evidences the early employment of confederacies for battle. Kederlaomer reigned over a confederacy with four other kings (14:2-4) for a twelve-year period before a revolution. Other primitive states were allied into military confederacies as well (14:6-11; 26:28). At about 2000 BC, Kederlaomer raided Sodom and captured Abram's nephew, Lot (14:12).

Prior to the military skirmish described in Genesis 14, Kederlaomer and the Eastern Confederation had conquered the five-nation Western Alliance. For a 12-year period, Kederlaomer—even though 600 miles to the east—had kept these city-states in check, likely by the combination of taxes and installed martial law. However, after 12 years of paying tribute, and perhaps with a relaxation of boots-on-the-ground political operatives, the cities of Palestine rebelled in the 13th year. They stopped paying taxes and sought to declare independence.

Kederlaomer allowed a one-year grace period, but marched on the Eastern Alliance in the 14th year (14:5). He marched through the desert with a large force and conquered another seven city states (14:5-7 records the details) enroute to reclaiming the five rebel states. In the process, he also encircled that Western Confederation, and breathed down their neck. Kederlaomer, to put it in context, was the ruler over at least 15 different city-states. He was likely the most powerful man of his day in the middle east, only rivalled by Pharaoh internationally.

This requires sophistication, organization, personal charisma, and an infrastructure to keep all the small nations in line. Kederlaomer was to be feared for sure.

When the Western army engaged in battle, they were routed (14:10); some of their leaders and retreating soldiers were stuck in the tar pits and slaughtered. It was a total military success. Kederlaomer was now the Emperor from the Persian Gulf to the Mediterranean Sea, north of Egyptian territory.

Of interest, Abram was not attacked during this military excursion, and his estate was left intact.

As a summary point, the notion of monarchy, whether by consent or force, is therefore an old form of government, especially for small states. If the state needs little administration and is not so intrusive as to necessitate large inspection, a monarchy (or patriarchy) seems to have been sufficient for administration. Abram also refused to enter into treaties with those around him, lest he become obliged to them (14:21-24). Treaties were already in use by 2,000 BC (21:22 ff.; 26:28). It appears, therefore, that the propriety of entering into covenanted relationships is acknowledged. The key criteria for treaties, thereafter, were religious and prudential factors. Several injunctions are issued to avoid treaties with parties who did not share belief in the one, true God. The basis of a treaty being either the guaranteed sufficiency of the human parties—a frail foundation—or based on an oath to God, the Lord's people should only expect treaties to be kept by those with a strong allegiance to God or some other supreme commitments.

Abram Conquers Kederlaomer

Abram is brought into this because he sensed a family obligation to rescue Lot, his nephew. While Lot had chosen to settle near Sodom, he did not resist the pull of that culture, gradually capitulating to that immorality. By the time of this conquest of Kederlaomer, Lot is now living in Sodom (14:12), surely a lesson not to allow oneself too much familiarity with an immoral culture. And Abram receives a report that his nephew and family have been conquered and taken captive.

Abram then called upon his own trained militia (14:14) and pursued the strongest king in the region, Kederlaomer, who seemed invincible. Abram and his security force (14:13), however, defeated the Kederlaomer alliance, chasing them as far north as Damascus and reclaiming Lot, his wives, and all his possessions (14:16). If one understands the incredible dominance of Kederlaomer, whose armies were numerous and whose weaponry must have been superior, for Abram to defeat him was one of the largest military victories in history.

While, some credit this enormous upset to the surprise tactic (it was at night) or to the division of Abram's troops, neither of those are sufficient to explain Abram's victory. The cause of the victory is later attributed to God himself (14:20), surely be the underlying cause.

Abram's blessings led to a large business and militia. While he was passing off his wife Sarai in Egypt, still his net worth increased greatly. By the middle of Genesis 13, Abram and Lot each had so many herds, flocks, workers, and family, that they required a subdivision of the land. At the end of his life, he had accumulated not only massive livestock herds, but he had a battalion of 318 trained soldiers who had been born into his household (14:14). That suggests that at least 20 years of development had occurred.

That private security force was evidently quite tactically proficient, as they allowed Abram to intimidate the largest powers of his day. Abram likely had other servants in his household as well. As these workers married and had families, it is not at all beyond question to think of "Abram Enterprises, Inc." as numbering in the thousands. If he had over 300 soldiers and another 100 workers (the shepherds and servants would likely outnumber the security force, although some of them pulled double-duty), if each of those 400 were married and had only 3 children (a small family for that era), that would amount to an enterprise of 2,000. And that enterprise grew over time. Abram, by chapters 14 of Genesis, must be viewed not only as a spiritual man, but as a prosperous businessman, who headed a sprawling business and farm. He had to be organized, and he was known as the head of this organization.

He devoted all his assets to reclaiming Lot—surely, an admirable trait showing his commitment to protect his family. In view of the greatness and awe of Emperor Kederlaomer, this victory over that military commander (14:17), even putting him in the unusual position of retreating, made Abram an instant celebrity. Abram, along with Lot and his possessions returned home.

As he did, two kings seek him out—one for a self-interested alliance, the other for spiritual blessing.

The king of Sodom (either he'd survived the tar pits retreat or this was a new one) approached Abram and sought an alliance—a smart move on his part. However, he wanted a share of the plunder, suggesting that Abram take the material possessions and allow him to retain as servants the human resources (14:21). Abram had the discernment to know not to enter into a league with this immoral man. He also realized that if God were to receive all the glory and tribute that he did not wish to risk allowing a human king to claim credit for any victory or conquest of Abram. Abram was wise enough to be sensitive to the likely claims for credit from the king of Sodom should he ally with him. Thus, Abram refused this proposed alliance.

Melchizedek: King and Priest

The other king who sought an alliance with Abram was Melchizedek, the king of Salem (later the area that became Jerusalem). This king—

his name means "king of righteousness," or from his region (Salem/Shalom), his name meant "king of peace"—was none other than a human leader, like all the other named kings.[5]

King Melchizedek was also a true believer, neither from the Hebrew line and long before Abram was an admired figure. This King approaches Abram, bringing the culinary items of a friendly feast—bread and wine—and has a meal celebrating this victory and likely establishing a treaty. Melchizedek, in contrast to the king of Sodom, was not merely seeking a treaty of convenience; he actually was spiritually one with Abram, worshipping the same God and already serving as a priest to *El Shaddai*, the Most High God (14:18).

Melchizedek not only brought the prototypes of what would later be elements for Holy Communion—no accident, but a preview provided by God—but he also blessed Abram and showed that they shared the same true faith. In his words of blessing, Melchizedek praised God as "most high," affirmed that God was Creator of heaven and earth (this is not evolutionary cosmology at this early date), and credited God for giving Abram this victory and for delivering him from his enemies (14:20). This short poem of praise shows true unity of the faith with Abram—in fact, it shows that Abram could learn from this king/priest of Salem, who was more advanced in the faith at this time.

The New Testament in Hebrews 7 develops more on Melchizedek as a righteous leader and as a type of priest who was not descended from Levi. He is of an eternal priestly order, as was Jesus.

Abram recognized his greatness by paying him a tribute of 10%. While Abram alone is credited with the military victory in these verses, on his own initiative, he wished to honor Melchizedek as his superior. That is the heart of tithing—when we give tribute to one who is superior to us and who owns us. Instead of paying a forced tax to a king hundreds of miles away, Abram wished to acknowledge the spiritual superiority of Melchizedek and thus freely gave him 10% of the plunder.

---

[5] The phrase 'without father, mother or genealogy' (Heb. 7:4) refers to the Levitical priesthood's requirement for familial descent, not that he was unborn or superhuman. The context identifies him as any other king, no more no less—except for his spiritual maturity.

Abram's Character, contrasted with the earlier event

In Genesis 14, as a contrast to the previous chapter, we see Abram as nothing but admirable. He is a prosperous and wise businessman; he is a military-tactical genius; he valued his kinfolks enough to risk fighting the most powerful man of his day; and he evidenced no hubris—paying tribute to Melchizedek who share the true faith. Abram is a hero in Genesis 14 in every way.

He is worthy of respect, even though far from perfect. The contrast shows us exemplary behavior and character. He will have other lapses coming, but we should not allow his imperfections to lead us to cast him aside. He is still Father Abraham, the father of all those who have true faith.

William Symington once helped capture the significance of remembering:

> We would not be chargeable with the enormous wickedness of forgetting that men are only what God makes them, and that to him all the glory ... is to be ascribed. But we are, at the same time, unable to see wherein the bestowment of a due need of praise on the memory of such ... contravenes any maxim of sound morality, or any dictate of inspiration. We ... have no hesitation in attempting to awaken, in the men of the present generation, sentiments of admiration and gratitude for the memory of worthies to whom all are so deeply indebted.... While we claim and exercise the right of bringing these, like all other human productions, to the infallible touchstone of Revelation.[6]

Cutting the Covenant

After this gigantic military victory and in view of the earlier promise from God that Abram's descendants would be a numerous as the grains of dust (13:16), Abram may have calmed down from the adrenaline rush and wondered if he'd heard God correctly. In Genesis 15, God will seek to reassure Abram and employ another example of magnitude, promising that his descendants will be as calculable as the number of stars in the sky.

---

[6] "Historical Sketch of the Westminster Assembly of Divines" by William Symington in *Commemoration of the Bicentenary of the Westminster Assembly of Divines* (Glasgow, 1843), 69, 71.

Abram, however, had a problem—an understandable one. How could he have a large family, if it could not even be started? Sarai was barren, and he was old. He questioned the Lord who reassured him in terms of the covenant God.

God reveals himself to Abram in this chapter as his shield, his very great reward (v. 1) and the one who led him out of Ur of the Chaldees (15:7). In typical covenant formulation, God identifies himself as the Sovereign, as Abram addressed him (vss. 2, 8). God, then, establishes a covenant sign to assure Abram of the truthfulness of his revelation. This is part one of the covenant, with the second part occurring in Genesis 17.

But Abram responded in faith. He believed God and it was credited to him as righteousness (15:6). This infamous verse is repeated in Romans 4 and Galatians 3. God's covenant method of salvation did not change over two millennia. Abram, even with his flaws, was included in God's covenant and viewed by God as if he'd never sinned or as if he's always been righteous. Since, he was not always righteous, we are correct to see that God saves him through a substitute who is in his place. Abram may have gotten several things wrong, but he got this right: trust God in what he reveals.

And even if what he reveals is unusual—more of that is to come for Abram!—the friend of God trusts him and follows. He may ask a few questions, but he doesn't over-question.

Abram believed God; he trusted him. Even with an odd ceremony, God was clear enough that Abram adhered to him and the covenant is in force. Still, scriptures portray this habit of a lively discussion with God. Abram at times is a questioning adherent of the Lord. The commendable thing about him is that he asks God questions—he was intimate enough to do so without condemnation—and he accepts God's answers, even if it takes a series of questions (see chap. 18). God did not rebuke Abram for asking twice in this chapter—the first time, "how can this be?" and the second time, "How can I be sure?" The realistic thing about Abram also is that while he obeyed, there were times that his 'inquiring mind' wanted to know things. Questioning is not always a sign of sinful doubt. Failure to obey is.

Abram, flawed though we might have been in some aspects, is still held up as a great hero of the faith in the New Testament (see Romans

4 and Heb. 11). Neither his questioning nor his lapses cancel his stature as father to all the faithful. Perhaps, we need to learn to rest in imperfect heroes, while still embracing what God does in them and for us. Lord Acton spoke of the past as capable of teaching by illuminating "the instructions derived from the errors of great men."[7] He also noted: "The value of history is its certainty—against which opinion is broken." If we find that our parents were on to some things that we have not realized, or if perhaps their insights were deeper than the average paperback Christian book, then we should not be so arrogant as to cling to an uncritical bias for the modern. Jeremiah spoke of the "ancient paths" (Jer. 6:16)—those tried and trusted ruts of life that rebels sought to re-fill because they were routine.

---

[7] J. Rufus Fears, ed., *Selected Writings of Lord Action: Essays in Religion, Politics, and Morality* (Indianapolis: Liberty Press, 1988), 623.

The Wrong Way to Build a Covenant Family (Genesis 16)

Sarai is another example of faith, who is praised by later saints. Yet, it would be another case of hagiolatry to think that she had no flaws or was justified in some of her actions.

Opposed to a determinism by caprice, Acton advised that "knowledge of history means choice of ancestors."[8] He differentiated between being governed by the past as opposed to a liberating knowledge gained from the past. He recommended: "Live both in the future and the past. Who does not live in the past does not live in the future." Acton, who spoke of progress as "the religion of those who have none,"[9] also noted that history "gives us the line of progress, the condition of progress, the demonstration of error."[10] Of this historical perspective, Acton cheered: "If it enables us to govern the future . . . by disclosing the secret of progress and the course sailed, the nation that knows the course best and possesses the most perfect chart will have an advantage over others in shaping the destiny of man."[11]

As we look at Genesis 16, we will have to be careful not to be crusaders for gender perfection either. Indeed, Sarai and Abram both take paths in this chapter that should not be copied at home.

Sarah is sometimes presented as a feminist heroine. She was a strong woman to be sure and admirable in many ways. A depiction of her as a glass-ceiling breaking feminist icon is a stretch, however, especially considering her consent to go along with the plan to

---

[8] J. Rufus Fears, ed., *Selected Writings of Lord Action: Essays in Religion, Politics, and Morality* (Indianapolis: Liberty Press, 1988), 620.
[9] Ibid., 636.
[10] Ibid., 634.
[11] Idem.

masquerade as Abram's sister (twice!) and the offering of her assistant, Hagar, to conceive a child with Abram.

Still, though, we should not forget that even with these aspects of her resume, she is commended as a model of faith. The New Testament, in fact, does see her as a heroine of faith.

Genesis chapter 16 will challenge us to view her with both respect and balance, and we should accept that challenge.

Thus far we have the following information about Sarai:
- In Genesis 11:29-31, she is introduced as Abram's wife, and we are informed that she was barren, as this family began their trek toward Haran and Canaan. She willingly relocates with Terah (her father-in-law), Abram, and Lot, and the family.
- Next, in Genesis 12:5, she is reported as moving with Abram and Lot toward Haran.
- Then, the end of Genesis 12 reports that nearly-disastrous wife-swap, in which Abram—to protect his life—allows Sarai to be taken into Pharaoh's palace as any other wife (and she cooperates). She is subjected to conditions that no one would advise—how willing she was to support this arrangement, we may never know. Notwithstanding, God delivers this family, and they move forward.
- Then, God tells Abram in Genesis 13:14-18 that he will have a family as numerous as the dust of the earth. Surely, Abram passed this on to Sarai.
- And in Genesis 15:2-5, when Abram wonders if God will provide descendants, there God promises that one would come from his own body and his family would be as numerous as the stars in the sky. Again, Abram passed this on to Sarai.

As chapter 16 opens, a problem is clear: Abram and Sarai cannot populate a family if they never can have the first child. Sarai is barren, and the couple have tried for many years to have a family. Sarai could well, by the time of conception, have been post-menopausal and unable to bear any child. Thus, the problem was that this family could never fulfill God's promise if they could not begin the chain of conception.

Accordingly, Sarai comes up with a plan—and even while we respect her, this plan is either humanism or pragmatism. It is a worldly attempt to accomplish some aspect of God's plan by using ungodly methods. And the form of this cycle of the narrative is that Sarai proposes, and Abram agrees. She is clearly suggesting, leading, and setting the tone for the family.

What she did in this Sin-drome

In this case, Sarai proposed a method of building the family that surely should not be tried at home. In fact, it is clear that she views herself as 'building' the covenant family, but it is so wrong-headed. She advocates, since she cannot conceive a child, that Abram proceed with the venture, and that he have intercourse with Sarai's Egyptian (likely acquired during the earlier Egyptian sojourn) handmaiden. Imagine, handing off (a) another woman for sexual reproduction to a man; and (b) providing your husband with an additional sexual partner?

Must I repeat? Don't try this at home.

Abram, then, plays the submissive husband. He agrees (and probably told all his buddies at the gym about this one), and follows Sarai's plan—even though Abram had already had this conversation with God about how the child of promise would come about. He likely agreed with something like the following: "Well, gee whiz, honey. Is that what you really want? Do you think this will work? I only want to make you happy with that cute, hot little . . . , I mean I'll be happy to do as you think best. Whatever you want."

Obviously, the above supplies details that are not in the Bible, but we can sure hear such being said.

Hagar, quickly becomes pregnant, and as soon as Sarai's plan succeeds, it is a disaster. That was Sarai's plan.

The various parts of the Sin-drome include at least the following:

a. Not relying on God's promise (clearly revealed in Gen. 15:4).
b. Adopting a marital configuration not condoned by God—and this should be a lasting reminder and warning to us to avoid having marriages with anything other than one male with DNA cells and one woman with DNA cells until death parts.
c. Role-reversals which prove quite contrary to God's plan.
d. Blame (16:5).

e. Jealousy—imagine that Hagar would detest Sarai (cf. also Proverbs 30:21-23), and that Sarai would think Hagar viewed her as "little in her eyes."
f. Retaliation-mistreatment.

Hagar flees (v. 6), and the second part of this chapter focuses on her. She is not looked down upon in this narrative. In fact, God comes to the rescue of this vulnerable young mother. Recalling that in this ancient society, Hagar would have had no rights, no legal protections, no recourses, makes it all the more dramatic that God sends an Angel to protect her.

This Angel of the Lord (cf. also in Gen. 21:17; 22:11; 31:11-13; Ex. 3:2; Numbers 22-24; and Judges 6:12) attends to this mistreated, exploited, and vulnerable maid-servant to Sarai. He finds her near a specific brook, and initiates a conversation, asking where she is from and where she's heading. He obviously knew.

She explains her predicament, and the Angel of the Lord—with the full authority of God, and not necessarily deity himself—assures her that God will provide. Further, he instructs her to do something that few would advise under similar circumstances: he tells her to return to Sarai and submit to her mistress. Few things could be harder or less imaginable. Yet, the short book of Philemon in the NT (NT is the abbreviation for New Testament) has a similar counsel. And the main character of the NT, Jesus, is also instructed to submit to the most extreme hardship possible. And as 1 Peter 2 shows, he did. God doesn't always deliver us from hardship, but he gives grace to bear up.

The Angel gives Hagar assurance, and she will name her son Ishmael, which means God hears. She knows that the Lord has heard her misery, and that her son will be a blessing. The Angel further promises that Hagar will also yield a huge family through Ishmael, even though he will be a wild donkey of a man and at enmity with virtually everyone in his life. Still, the Angel delivers Hagar, comforts her, and gives her promise. And for 13 years, after she returns, every time the name "Ishmael" is used in Abram's compound, a dagger pierced Sarai's heart. For Hagar had a son, and Sarai didn't. In addition, a veneer of spiritual superiority is also embedded into this name. Hagar could boast that God heard her—not Sarai—and the little ruffian would sire a large family, too.

But this is not the child of promise, which will await the next chapters in Genesis.

The New Testament on Sarai

But don't minimize the role and faith of Sarah. It is she who is championed in the NT. Hebrews 11:11-12 commends her, along with Abraham, for living by faith. It may be a challenge as I said at the outset of this chapter, but should we not learn to view our heroes, even with their flaws, but not rejecting their traits that are worthy of imitation?

Consider to how Galatians 4:21-31 contrasts Hagar and Sarah, and clearly commends Sarah to us—so watch the Sarah-bashing or thinking that we are morally superior.

Building upon these Old Testament (hereafter, OT or NT) narratives (actually from Gen. 16 to Gen. 21), the earlier texts are confirmed as historic and reliable (Gal. 4:22-23). Then, however, the apostle Paul draws a larger lesson from this history. Hagar and Sarah each represent a city, according to this early epistle in the NT. Hagar and her children symbolize the physical Jerusalem of the day (ca. 45 AD); this set of descendants are termed slaves (4:25), but in contrast, there is a Jerusalem that is above (4:26), which is the city of those who are liberated. The children of promise, stemming from Isaac (4:28), are true believers, and Hagar's children are not the role models to follow.

Through it all, it is the children of Sarah who are the true heirs of God's promises, leading to this lesson: "Therefore, brothers we are not children of the slave woman, but of the free woman."

Sarah wins out in the end, and she joins Abram as a spiritual parent for all true faith (cf. also Rom. 4:11-12).

Flawed People?

We are seeing a theme develop, beginning with the patriarch Abraham: some of these heroes of the faith are fairly flawed. That accurate observation gives rise both to realism about our spiritual ancestors and also to comfort among imperfect saints.

Let me briefly review a few examples of this from some of the chapters of early human history in the Book of Genesis.

- After Abram is called by God to leave his native land and family to relocate to Canaan, a famine arises, and he must temporarily move to Egypt to survive. When he does so, he realizes that his wife is beautiful and that he might be killed so that some other man could take her as his wife. So, Abram concocts a story—that is often rationalized but that is clearly deceitful. Abram is greatly to be admired, but not only does he do this once . . . but he repeats this again later in Genesis 20. Pretty flawed, right?
- As Abram and Lot are being blessed by the Lord, they decide to split up since one tract of land cannot support both of their growing enterprises and families. Lot chooses to move closer to the very immoral town of Sodom—eventually settling there. He will later need a dramatic rescue but will lose his wife to the lure of loose living in the process.
- In Genesis 15, Abram questions God twice and asks for a confirming sign. He does "believe God" (15:6) and is justified, but some explanations were needed first.
- God clearly told Abram that the child of promise would come from his DNA. After 10 years of such not happening, Sarai concocts her own plan and lends her maidservant, Hagar, to Abram to start the family line. Not surprisingly, this does not end up very well. Jealousy arises, Abram submits to his wife's immoral plan, and God will keep his promise by bringing about Isaac when both Abram and Sarai are very old. So flawed, that you don't want to try this at home.
- Sarai even receives a slight name change because when she overhears God and Abram discussing how the Lord will bring about a child of promise, Sarai bursts out into laughter. It is not the laughter of comic joy—instead it is the guffaw of disbelief.

No, all these examples were not perfect. And that does not include later a mom's ruse with Jacob and Esau, a wife of Pharaoh who framed an innocent young man of sexual harassment, a tricky Jacob, a dad who subs a daughter in for another on her wedding night, and brothers who loathe Joseph so much that they rid themselves of him by selling him into slavery. Yes, our Old Testament heroes were flawed people.

Guess what? When we come to the New Testament we see the same, especially in the gospel accounts.

- Peter boasts that he will never desert Jesus, but he races like a scared toddler when the pressure gets turned up.
- The other disciples run or fall asleep in Jesus' greatest moment of need—one young disciple even seeks to avoid arrest by dashing out of his toga.
- Those Sons of Thunder grow . . . quiet and timid only after time.
- Later, Paul is not perfect, and many segments of the New Testament church are not what we wish to imitate—consider the Corinthian church in 1 Corinthians 5-6!

So, do we give up, if our churches are not filled with perfected saints?

I hope not—for that would close more doors than even the most Spartan government's restrictions, and it would also contradict many biblical examples. Our faith encompasses flawed people.

So, as we study our Bibles, let's continue to be realistic—and also not allow ourselves to be deceived that we are morally superior, suggesting that "We would never sin" in some such area. The truth is that Jesus did and does receive sinners still.

In view of flawed disciples—then and now—that's why I love the words to this hymn: "Jesus Sinners Doth Receive."

*"When a helpless lamb doth stray, after it, the Shepherd, pressing
Through each dark and dang'rous way, brings it back, his own possessing.
Jesus seeks thee, O believe: Jesus sinners doth receive."*

*"Oh, how blest it is to know: were as scarlet my transgression,
It shall be as white as snow by the blood and bitter passion;
For these words I now believe; Jesus sinners doth receive."*

Doubt and Miracle—Abraham and Sarah Laughing (Genesis 17, 18)

C. S. Lewis reflected a hearty perspective similar to the one in this present work. In *God in the Dock*, he found himself highly skeptical of several modernistic notions. In his essay, "Dogma and the Universe," he spoke to a common scandal in the words below.

> It is a common reproach against Christianity that its dogmas are unchanging, while human knowledge is in continual growth. Hence, to unbelievers, we seem to be always engaged in the hopeless task of trying to force the new knowledge into molds which it has outgrown. I think this feeling alienates the outsider much more than any particular discrepancy . . . For it seems to him clear that, if our ancestors had known what we know about the universe, Christianity would never have existed at all.[12]

In his chapter "On the Reading of Old Books," he made a number of key observations. Decrying the habit of initially turning to secondary sources rather than primary sources, Lewis thought it was "topsy-turvy" to maintain a "preference for the modern books and this shyness of the old ones."[13] Yet, he noted the great prevalence of this modern philia in theological circles. Whereas, Lewis preferred to have the reader first attend to the direct sources (with whatever guidance was necessary), he found a trend that substituted rumor for primary sources.

Lewis continued with a metaphor about entering the play after intermission. He asserted that if one enters a discussion group at 11:00, without knowing what has gone on from 8:00-11:00, one may interpret many things out of context. Inside jokes, laughter, references, and other nuances will not be appreciated. In the same way, Lewis continued, "you may be led to accept what you would have indignantly rejected if

---

[12] C. S. Lewis, *God in the Dock* (Grand Rapids: Eerdmans, 1970), 38.
[13] Lewis, op. cit., 201.

you knew its real significance."[14] The "only safety," according to Lewis, was to hold to the standard of plain ("mere" as the puritan Richard Baxter called it) Christianity "which puts the controversies of the moment in their proper perspective." This approach preserves a crucial perspective that is often wanting amidst today's ideological forays.

Lewis recommended the classics, the great books of Christianity. Lewis correctly saw the danger of holding the past in contempt and called for a fresh acquaintance with the best of the past. I, too, want to concur with Lewis and others who have realized this. The theology of an earlier day has much to teach us. We might begin by admitting that there is a beam in our own eye—our presumption that we have superior insight. Regular dosage of history may cure us of some presumptiveness.

As we arrive at Genesis 17, God finalizes the covenant with Abram. The Lord reiterates the terms of this covenant-agreement as "walk before me blamelessly," and establishes the sign of circumcision as the mark of covenant continuation. Walking before God blamelessly is not sinless perfectionism so much as it is keeping the covenant with integrity.

It becomes clear that the Abram-Hagar-Ishmael line is not the line of promise (cf. also Gal. 4:21-31 above). Rather, God will provide a covenant family from Abram and Sarai—hard as it may be to believe. It's well worth a short review to see how God works in all this.

The Lord reiterated to Abram that he would make him a great nation. God's identity was as "El Shaddai," and he charged Abram with walking before him blamelessly. El Shaddai also told Abram that he would have many descendants. To confirm this, he issued a name-change for Abram ("exalted father"). A name change also indicated that the Namer was the superior (as in Gen. 2, when Adam names the animals and even Eve). Henceforth, he would be called Abraham, which meant "the father of multitudes." Further, all his neighbors would mock him for this name change, since he was thus far unable to start his family with a single heir.

---

[14] Idem.

Yes, at the age of 99, God would start this amazing family (17:1). Sarai was a decade younger but well past the child-bearing age. In this covenant renewal, God promised to provide the land of Canaan (v. 8) and many children.

The sign of this covenant was circumcision for every male (including those who were not Jewish, cf. vss. 12c-13) on the 8th day. There were no exceptions allowed, and if one was not circumcised, he would be cut off (a pun?) from the people as a covenant breaker (17:14). By this sign, the Lord wished to have dedicated even the reproductive organ, so thorough was God's call on a life.

Sarai also received a minor name change at this point; she was a "princess" who would become "the mother of nations; kings of people will come from her." (17:16)

At this point, a key term enters the narrative: *laughs*. For at this incredible revelation, Abraham could stand in seriousness no longer. He fell facedown—a sign of both surrender and the inability to resist—and he "laughed," thinking to himself that there was no way a son would be born to a man nine months later, after he turned 100 years of age.

Abraham could not logically see what the Lord told him as possibly coming about. It seemed impossible, biologically and in every way. He countered again that perhaps Ishmael could just be the child of promise. I imagine the Lord could have rolled his eyes and said, "Abe, we've been over this." And God confirmed precisely that his plan was to use Sarai to bear a son—and Ishmael would have his own blessing.

After this conversation, the Lord "went up," and Abraham obeyed. He (at age 99), Ishmael (at age 13), and all the males in his household-enterprise were circumcised. In the end, Abraham obeyed.

But Abraham had laughed—and he was not the only one who would laugh. Yet, Sarai's laughter would be more prominent and even rebuked.

Still the Lord continued his covenant with Abraham. In Genesis 18, he visited Abraham—who was a solicitous host, quickly preparing a meal for three visiting men, who the account later makes clear were God plus two angels. As Abraham shows incredible hospitality, the Lord enquires about where Sarai is. Abraham answers that she is in the tent (18:9), and God promises to return in about a year and Sarah will give birth to a son. Guess what name this son of promise will receive?

"He laughs" or Isaac. In that case, however, the laughter may be caused by joy—the joy of finally receiving a son after 100 years of living.

However, Sarah is eavesdropping in Genesis 18:10. When she hears this promise, she is reminded of her age and that she is past the child-bearing age. So how does she react? Not exactly like Mary in the NT who said: "I am the handmaiden of the Lord. Let it be as you say." Instead, Sarah laughed (18:12), applying the same logic that Abraham had earlier, thinking that she was old and worn out and that this pleasure was simply too impossible.

God is in the process of teaching that nothing is impossible with him or too hard for him.

God, then confronts Sarah over her incredulity. In a candid exchange, the Lord asks Sarah why she laughed at this revealed plan—it is clear that God did not think of her laughter as a response of belief. She, then, made the mistake of Adam, Cain, and others in this early history: she denied the truth of what had happened. She said—like a child caught disobeying her parent—"Not me; I didn't do it. I did not laugh." (18: 13-14) And God did not permit that to stand; he corrected, "yes, you did laugh." The Lord didn't think it was a good time for laughter.

Abraham and Sarah both laughed, thinking the promised miracle was ridiculous.

Even some of the greatest saints—in this case, the mother of nations and kings of people—burst into laughter at one of God's revealed plans. Sarah thought it laughable that she at 90 and Abraham at 100 could start a family after all these years. She didn't merely wonder quietly or think of alternatives—instead, she went beyond doubting and found the prospect that God would do to be laughed at.

But let's don't throw her away totally. Later, the NT holds her up as an example of faith, and Galatians 4 contrasts her with Hagar. Our great grandparents may have been doubters at times, they may have initially reacted in skepticism, they may have asked for repeated signs, but when they keep God's covenant, we should imitate their faith.

The Lord does not seem to kick them to the curb as quickly as we might—unless we tragically allow our moral superiority to govern.

Abraham, The Negotiator (Genesis 18)

I'll start with this statement and end this chapter with the same: Abraham, even with him occasional bumbling, was a giant of faith and a friend of God. The latter half of Genesis 18 depicts him as thinking that he is negotiating with God, bringing the Lord's previously determined will down to what Abraham would think of as more reasonable.

He meant well. He even thought that part of his duty was to protect and name and honor of God. And in this section, he thought that God's judgment might be a bit too severe. Thus, he engages in a negotiation—much like any human would have with an employer or another human authority. However, in truth he neither changes God's mind nor does he persuade God to be more compassionate. The error is that God is compassionate aplenty—and he never needs our coaching. Ever.

Abraham was, in addition to his other successes, a fine negotiator. He was accustomed to bargaining for cattle, land, resources, and workers—why, on occasion he even used Sarah as a bargaining chip. And previously, he had attempted to negotiate with God to allow another son to be the heir. Twice (in Gen. 15 and in Gen. 17), despite knowing God's decision and will on a key matter—namely, that he would have a biological son with Sarah at old age—Abraham sought to make suggestions, which he thought might be helpful to the Almighty. He asked God to allow Ishmael, his son with Hagar, to promulgate the line of descendants. The Lord clearly did not agree to such bargaining.

In the first part of Genesis 18, three guests had arrived. All had a human appearance. One was God, the other two were angels, but all three assumed human form. Abraham raced to show generous hospitality to these three. He asked Sarah to make a lavish meal, and when the Lord inquired about Sarah's whereabouts, Abraham explained she was in the tent making the meal. This Divine Person promised that in a year (18:11), he would return and Sarah would have the greatly desired and miraculously conceived son. Sarah cracked up, thinking this was utterly impossible. The Lord, then, corrected her for her unbelief.

From there, the narrative continues. In verses 16-17 of Genesis 18, two of the three guests head toward Sodom (we will meet them again in Gen. 19:1 ff), and Abraham is left alone with God. God treats Abraham as a true friend, almost a partner, and says that he should not hide from Abraham what he is about to do.

What God is about to do is to investigate first-hand to see if the wickedness of Sodom is as bad as reported. An "outcry" against Sodom had arisen to the courts of heaven, pleading with the true judge of the world, to fix or judge Sodom—so wicked was she. And the outcry was likely not from those of Sodom. More likely it was from others who had business dealings there or who had passed through that city.

God then treats Abraham as a friend, almost a colleague, asking aloud, "shall I hide from Abraham" what I'm about to do? The Lord did not have to take Abraham into his counsel, but as we will repeat, Abraham was a friend of God. And note that the ensuing conversation does not show the Divine Person rebuking or correcting the human for the following questioning.

This narrative is recorded for our instruction (1 Cor. 10:6, 11), and it teaches us not only about who God truly is but also about human limits. Unfortunately, some people act as though they may plead with God, persuade him, or somehow convince him to alter his plans and change his mind. I believe this lively conversation is recorded to teach us the opposite.

So, as we discuss these briefly, you might ask yourself this question: Is it good to try to change God's mind? That is what Abraham thought he was doing. We will see that God did not change his plan in the least.

The Attempted Negotiation

After it becomes clear that God will investigate the "outcry" against Sodom and will likely destroy that city-state, Abraham engages in a conversation to seek to have God spare Sodom because of the presence of some. His real question seems to be: Will the Judge of all the earth fail to distinguish between the good and the evil, sweeping away even the righteous with the mass of the unrighteous?

Abraham pleads with God six different times to bring down—so he thinks—the threshold that will prevent Sodom from destruction. He begins, acknowledging God's greatness and bargains that if as few as 50 righteous people are in Sodom, will God not spare that place. The Lord answers that he will spare Sodom if there are 50 people present. He knew there were not.

Abraham then proceeds as if at a flea-market, asking if the small differential of 5 additional persons would make a difference. In other words, he asked, if only 45 righteous live there, would God not spare Sodom? The Lord agreed on this second benchmark that he would not destroy Sodom if 45 righteous people were there.

Then, a third benchmark is mentioned by Abraham, if as few as 40 righteous people were there—and Abraham begins to realize that he is out on a limb asking repeatedly—would God not spare Sodom? God agrees not to destroy if there were 40—and he knew perfectly well that such agreement would cause no alteration of his plans.

But Abraham thought he was helping God's reputation and also that he was coaching the Lord just a tad to be merciful. One of the main lessons to learn from this chapter is this: Never think that you are merciful than God or that you need to coach him just a bit in compassion.

Next, Abraham asks—if this won't offend—if 30 righteous people were there, would God not spare Sodom. The Lord consented—but note from the end of this episode how he did not change his plan.

Yet, a 5th time, Abraham—and he realizes along the way that he is pushing the limits, approaching the edges of acceptable boldness—asks if God will spare the region if as few as 20 righteous people lived in Sodom. Abraham likely is feeling pretty good about his arbitration skills; yet he knows he cannot ask much more. He's already overextended any reasonable negotiation.

Still, he asks one more bold time: what if as few as 10 righteous people live in Sodom, will not the judge of all the earth distinguish the righteous from the unrighteous and spare some. To this also, the Lord consents.

From the outcome (see Gen. 19:27-28), it becomes clear that God did destroy Sodom. She was so entirely corrupt that it would be an injustice to allow her to continue, so perverse, so corrupt was her society. And not only were there not even 10 righteous there, but when the Angels instruct Lot to flee (Gen. 19:11ff), he gathers up his two daughters and wife, and he invites the two future sons-in-law to accompany him, but they mock and laugh at the absurdity of leaving such a cool city (and are destroyed in it). The sum total of righteous who flee from Sodom is four (not 50, not 45, not 40, not 30, not 20, not 10), and one of those is lost in transit as she turned back to look lovingly on Sodom. Luke will later instruct in a short but packed verse: "Remember Lot's wife." (Lk 17:32)

Accordingly, there were no more than three righteous people in Sodom, and that count is pretty generous when you read the end of this episode in Genesis 19—the gals were hardly exemplary.

God hardly changed his mind. He did exactly what he'd planned to do. And his vivid narrative teaches us. While Abraham is not rebuked for this attempted negotiation, it is also recorded to teach us how God knows what is ahead, plans what happens, and is not such a puny God as to be persuaded by us (cf. sometime review Isaiah 40 on this).

The Flawed Assumptions

Abraham's attempted bartering may now be analyzed. He made several mistakes in this, and one of the reasons for this being recorded is to teach us by a negative example. This is another of those "Don't try this at home!" sections of Genesis.

Abraham had at least three flawed assumptions.

First, he assumed that there must be some innate human goodness in every city—at least enough that God should not totally destroy it. Surely, he thought to himself, there were some good people. Surely, there would be 50 or 40 or 30 or 10 decent folks there. He makes a judgment based on the outward appearance of innate righteousness or presumed righteousness that was contrary to fact. He honestly thought that his input to God at this critical juncture was needed. He was quite wrong.

Second, he committed the fallacy of applying general statistics where they did not fit. It is quite easy to read any survey and take the percentages and apply those to every situation. However, life is so complex that this seldom works out. One may take any given statistical report, and if all variables are not the same, to import an inapplicable statistic to a situation where it does not fit will be to confuse issues and adopt wrong solutions. For example, during the Covid19 pandemic, all kinds of statistical generalizations were made, but people gradually had to drill down and apply statistics to situations that fit instead of imposing statistical models onto examples that were not identical.

Abraham assumed that surely, as stats reported, there must be at least some righteous people in Sodom. God uses this long arbitration to show that wrong statistical models are not helpful.

Third, Abraham assumed that he was more of a champion for righteousness than God. He thought—based on his errors above—that God might be behaving just a little bit too wrathful. Abraham meant well—and the Lord patiently endured his counsel—but Abraham was not more compassionate than God. The father of our faith did not know as accurately as God, and the friend of God did not successfully plea God down to changing his mind or plan.

No, God did what he'd planned all along. God knew the exact number of righteous in Sodom—and he knows the same in all cities (cf. Acts 18:10), and while Abraham thought he was assisting, advising, pleading for mercy, and helping God's image, he was incorrect. These verses teach us and warn us about such.

So back to prayer and persuasion. Do you have the view of prayer that if you can ask God enough and coach him enough, he will eventually—even if begrudgingly—bend to give you what you ask? Is that what happened here? Is God such a puny deity that he is persuaded by us?

Or ask about prayer these three questions after reviewing this chapter:

1. Does God change his mind? And see Malachi 3:6.
2. Do we influence God to change his mind? See Isaiah 40:14 ff.
3. Do we sometimes *think* we influence him to change his mind, only to realize that the Sovereign of the universe knows all things and does all things well (review Romans 8:28).

Abraham intended to do well. He had an extremely close relationship with God. Yet, neither Abraham nor any human being intercedes to alter the perfect, divine will of God. The Lord wanted people to know his sovereignty so that when they sought to treat God like a trading partner at a bazaar, they might consider this narrative first and take a more humble posture, praying or singing:

> *Whatever my God ordains is right;*
>   *His holy will abideth;*
> *I will be still whatever he doth,*
>   *And follow where he guideth.*
> *He is my God,*
>   *though dark my road*
> *He holds me that I shall not fall,*
>   *Wherefore to him I leave it all.*

Abraham, even with him occasional bumbling, still was a giant of faith and a friend of God.

Loving the City of Man:
Sodom Never Ends up Gay (Genesis 19).

The 19th chapter of Genesis flows from the previous chapter; it also presents a woeful picture of loving a city too much.

The two angels continue to Sodom, informed by God's assessment of their immorality. God knew that there were only a handful of his people in that city—and even among the four who would initially escape, those were not all-stars.

As the angels arrive in Sodom, Lot (Abraham's nephew) was sitting at the place of civic importance—"at the city gate." He may have been a lower level community leader of some sort. As he sees these two guests arrive, he recognizes that they are different—they are not normal men. He wishes to protect them from the ravages of rampant promiscuity. So, he invites them into his own home, prepares a simple meal (in contrast to the generous over-the-top hospitality of Abraham in the previous chapter), and urges them not to go outside. At first, the guests express their intent to reconnoiter the city, but they eventually accept his hospitality.

Before long, word spreads that there are new guests at Lot's house. The citizenry turns out and presses Lot to let these guests outside so that they may have sex with them (v. 5). The language of this chapter stresses that from young to old—a synecdoche (a part standing for the whole)—the whole city was saturated with the immoral norms. Lot has enough remaining moral sensibility to know that such would be wrong.

However, he shows the effect of acclimating too much to an immoral city by offering his virgin daughters to the homosexual gang. Not only is Lot not the "Father of the Year" for this wicked idea, but his enchantment with the city of Sodom is growing more and more apparent. At first, he separated from Abraham, choosing the fertile plain for business reasons. Over time, he grew more and more in step with Sodom. Like the proverbial frog-in-the-kettle, now he is participating in civic affairs at the city gate. Moreover, he has become accustomed to making moral compromises—imagine offering one's daughters for rape[15] to appease a lustful group of insistent perverts!

Furthermore, when he attempts to gather his family—his own future sons-in-law ridicule him for his old-fashioned morality and the notion that God might actually judge Sodom.

These angels do not allow Lot to follow through on this moral compromise and strike all the assailants blind (vss. 10-11). The angels then instruct Lot to gather any of his family and prepare to leave quickly. That is when the fiancees do not take such an old-fashioned notion seriously, thinking that Lot is somehow joking (v. 14). Can't we sense how far the moral infection is affecting Lot?

But there's more. The sons-in-law mock him and will not flee with his family in this exodus. No more than four people left Sodom, and Lot wasn't the only one in love with the city. His wife, who had been ordered not to turn back (v. 17), did look back on Sodom fondly and was turned into a pillar of salt (v. 26). She loved too much the libertinism, the commerce, the free-wheeling ethos of the city of man. And she was so caught up in it that she died for her love for that community.

---

[15] Victor Hamilton, *The Book of Genesis* (Eerdmans [1990, 1995] *NICOT*, 34-35) argues: We see at least four problems with the view that the prohibition here is only on homosexual rape. *First*, nowhere in the OT does the verb *yada'* have the nuance of "abuse" or "violate." *Second*, the OT uses unmistakable language to relate rape incidents. Thus, the Shechemites "seized" and "lay with" and "humbled" Dinah (Gen. 34:2). Amnon "forced and "lay with" his half-sister Tamar (2 Sam. 13:14). Similarly, the biblical laws about rape also use these terms: "seize," "lie with" (Dt. 22:25-27). *Third*, this interpretation forces one meaning on "know" in v. 5 (i. e., "abuse") but a different meaning on "know" three verses later (i.e., "have intercourse with"), for it is unlikely that Lot is saying: "I have two daughters who have never been abused." *Fourth*, such an interpretation forces these incredible words in Lot's mouth: "Do not rape my visitors. Here are my daughters, both virgins—rape them." Clearly, then, the incident frowns on homosexual relations for whatever reason.

Yes, it is possible to love the allure of a city so much that we lose our lives in it. That's why Jesus warned about gaining the whole world only to lose one's life.

Lot also was pretty attracted to this city. Even though God instructed him to flee far from it, he sought to do a little of that negotiation with God. He requested only to escape to Zoar, because he was too old to travel as far as God said. Nevertheless, God had mercy on Lot (v. 16), and permitted this short-term solution. Eventually, Lot and his two daughters—a total of three righteous (cf. 18:32) but the degree of moral compromise is stunning in these three—escape to a cave.

Then, the daughters, who had also become quite ethically elastic, sought to perpetuate the family line through their own father. Their incestuous idea didn't seem to hit many speed bumps. They decided to get Lot drunk (and he didn't seem too resistant), and on consecutive nights the older and then the younger of the two daughters have sex with their father and conceive children with him—all to continue a family line. Of course, they could have waited and found other males, but they quickly opted for this immorality, even callously naming one of the sons the equivalent of "From father" (Moab).

Surely, we must recollect the degenerative influence of loving and living in an immoral community. *It does have an effect.* Lot followed much of the moral decline that will be itemized in Romans 1. The root of his problem was that he valued the comforts, supposed freedom, business opportunities, and excitement of a city of man to the City of God. In contrast, Abraham will later be described as seeking another city (Heb. 11:14-16).

Abraham loved the eternal city, not the city that gave him pleasure and profit. Lot and most of his family chose the world. And "Remember Lot's wife" is one of the shorter verses in the NT (Luke 17:32). It warns us about turning toward the city of Man, about our attachments to it.

Sodom Never Ends Gay

The sin that triggered God's fiery judgment was the rampant sexual immorality. The various NT commentaries (Jude 4, 7; 2 Peter 2) make this crystal clear. To be sure, there were other besetting sins as mentioned by Ezekiel (cf. Ez. 16); however, Sodom achieved infamy for homosexuality—and various attempts to minimize that should not distract readers from that clear message.

In fact, all throughout the Bible, this sin is portrayed as much more than an alternative lifestyle or a private matter between consenting adults in one's own bedroom. This sin is consistently treated as wrong and contrary to nature itself. Leviticus chapter 18 has a list of sexual relationships to avoid—most within one or two links in a family. Adultery is condemned, and homosexuality is singled out as adultery in Leviticus 18:22 and 20:13. These were not sins to be tolerated.

Further, the New Testament condemns homosexual sex strongly. As part of a societal decline (note, the emphasis of v. 27 is that females might be expected to be more reserved in blatant sexual decline, but "even" women exchanged normal relations for abnormal ones), homosexual relations are condemned—not condoned or mitigated—in strong terms in Romans 1:26-28, being called "unnatural," "perverse," "detestable" (from Leviticus), and sinful. God's opinion on this subject is both clear and unchanging; it is also the most loving attitude toward sin for all eras and all families.

Later, Paul will write to Timothy and others, singling out homosexual offenders and the effeminate as sinful (1 Tim. 1:10; 1 Cor. 6:9). Notwithstanding, the teaching of Christianity is also that once a person is a true Christian, one is changed, washed, sanctified. "Once *were* some of you," Paul writes to the Corinthian church, but their identity was changed. Correct understanding of God's ways is that even the most potent and systemic of sins may be conquered and altered by the powerful working of the Holy Spirit. God, in conversion and sanctification, brings us back into alignment with nature by grace. He does not want his people remaining in perversion or unnatural sexual relationships.

Sadly, many churches and Christians have told themselves that it is loving to condone these relationships that God calls immoral—perhaps in the hopes of being inclusive or hospitable. However, the God who made us knows better and advises differently. It is a sign of advanced moral compromise to legitimate homosexuality or treat that desire as something that God made—especially when he so clearly classifies it as against nature and a lustful perversion in Romans 1.

As one commentator puts it: "They rape the mind, emotions, and body, trivializing the sacred, and legitimize the vulgar." (Waltke) No, Sodom does not end up gay; or at least it does not end up happy.

There are numerous attempts to explain away Sodom as not related to homosexuality. Some seek to revise the record to teach that the real issue was rudeness. These advocates allege the problem as being bad hospitality or seeking to force themselves on the visiting guests. Victor Hamilton, below, puts that to rest. Others seeks to partially mitigate homosexuality by drawing attention away from it, noting that Ezekiel 16 also accuses Sodom of pride and oppressing the poor. That is true, as well, but in no way does that minimize their sexual immorality. Still others, seek to explain that consensual homosexuality is fine, but this episode features non-consensual sex. All of these miss the mark and are but excuses to avoid the clear teaching in the Old Testament.

But in our feverish search to flee God's norms, many people have sought to carve out a safe space for same-sex marriage. A recent article by Alan Shlemon sums it up well. He notes that those who seek to legitimate homosexuality claim that only a kind of homosexuality is condemned, "only abusive, coercive, or exploitive forms. For example, the Bible condemns homosexual gang rape (e.g., Sodom and Gomorrah), master-slave sodomy, and pederasty (men who have sex with boys). These are obviously sinful acts involving abusive forms of homosexual sex."

Liberal interpreters seek to teach that there is a non-abusive, non-exploitive, or non-coercive kind of homosexual sin that is just fine. Thus, they invent a new sin. Shlemon describes:

> Rather, it's the kind of homosexuality that's expressed within loving, consensual relationships between gay men or lesbian women. Since the vast majority of modern-day same-sex relationships are characterized by mutual love, consent, and non-exploitive behavior, the biblical prohibitions don't apply to these modern expressions of love.
>
> Notice what pro-gay theology advocates have done. They've invented a new type of sin. They've taken an existing sin (homosexual sex) and divided it up into two flavors: sinful homosexual sex and non-sinful homosexual sex—a distinction foreign to the corpus of Scripture. It's no

longer homosexual sex that's sin. It's *abusive* homosexual sex that's sin. The added adjective is a qualifier that creates a new sin. Now, people can allegedly sidestep the biblical prohibition against homosexual sex.

He concludes:

> The problem with such a distinction is that it's foreign to Scripture. The Bible doesn't condemn a particular kind of homosexual acts. It simply condemns homosexual acts. For example, notice the straightforward reading of Leviticus 18:22: "You shall not lie with a male as one lies with a female; it is an abomination." There's nothing in the text that suggests that this banned behavior is only referring to abusive or exploitive homosexual sex. It is a simple prohibition against homosexual sex. The verse before forbids sacrificing your children to Molech, and the verse after prohibits bestiality. Therefore, nothing even in the context suggests Leviticus 18:22 is limited to abusive, coercive, or exploitive homosexuality. Neither is there an exception made for loving, consensual relationships. It's just a categorical prohibition against homosexual sex proper.
>
> The same is true of Lev. 20:13, Rom. 1:26–27, 1 Cor. 6:9–11, and 1 Tim. 1:9–11. None of these verses makes a distinction between abusive and loving homosexual sex. Pro-gay theology attempts to invent a new type of sin in order to sidestep an existing sin. That's a recent invention.[16]

Going against God's created nature never ends up well. Neither dalliances with immorality that prevails in certain communities, nor settled rejection of God's order, is blessed.

---

[16] "Pro-Gay Theology Invents a New Sin" by Alan Shlemon 02/09/2021; web posted at: https://www.str.org/w/what-does-the-bible-say-about-homosexuality-

Routine Ruses, Embarrassing Excuses: 'Take my wife, please.' (Genesis 20-21A)

Because of the similarity between this and chapter 12:10-20, some theorize that this is not true or that the accounts are being fabricated. Liberals have long and often sought errors in the Bible (Rom. 3:4). Some suggest that the Bible is a clumsy collection, pasted together by poor editors. The allegation is that the editors were so inept that they contradicted themselves or repeated themselves without even being aware. However, a better interpretation is that this sham is a repetition; it is genuinely a recurrence of Abraham's earlier mistake.

The chapter follows on the heels of the destruction of Sodom, along with an exhibition of the declining morality of Lot and his family. As Abraham travels through Gerar, he and Sarah agree (again!) to pose as siblings instead of spouses. Having no biological children made this possible. Twenty-five years after this first ruse, Sarah is evidently still attractive.

Abimelech—a common name for "prince" or literally, "my father is king"—is the ruler of the city-state of Gerar. He takes Sarah into his court, but God intervenes in a dream, warning him not to have a sexual relationship with Sarah, for she is married. Abimelech had not known this and pleads his innocence in a conversation recorded in these verses. God does not condemn him since he'd not acted immorally. Abimelech, almost quoting an earlier line from Abraham, calls on God not to judge the innocent in wrath if they've not committed wrong.

To grasp some of the drama of this narrative, see the comparison below between Ruse 1.0 and 2.0 (will there be a 3.0? Surely not!?)

48   *Scandals, Scoundrels, Deception and Depravity*

RUSE 1.0, CHAPTER 12	**RUSE 2.0, CHAPTER 20**
1. Preceded by Call of Abram Lot's errors	Preceded by Destruction of Sodom;
2. Famine caused relocation to Egypt (10)	Settles between Kadesh & Shur: Gerar (1)
3. 'When the Egyptians see you' (12,14)	Unstated by "She is my sister." (2)
4. Pharaoh takes her into palace (15)	Abimelech, King of Gerar took her,
5. Sex with Pharaoh (19)?	Abimelech innocent (4-6)
6. Abraham prospered by this (16)	Abraham, prophet and prayer (7)
7. Disease preempts (17)	Death threatened if disobedient (8)
8. Pharaoh confronts the patriarch (18)	Abimelech confronts the patriarch (9-10)
	Multiple levels of rationalization given (11-13)
	Abimelech showers gifts (14-16)
9. Pharaoh expels (19b-20)	Abimelech invites him to stay (15)
	Abraham blesses people, cures barrenness (18)

Abimelech returns Sarah to Abraham without incident. However, he also confronted Abraham (vss 9-10), asking him repeatedly why he did this and why he put Abimelech in such a precarious position. Abraham, the father in the faith, was scolded by a king from an unbelieving city, who was morally superior in this instance to Abraham and Sarah.

Abraham even sought to present several excuses for his immorality. Like Adam (Gen. 3), like Abraham earlier (Gen. 12), and like Sarah who would not initially admit her mocking laughter, Abraham would have been wiser to hang his head and quickly admit guilt. Instead, in the pattern that is becoming to frequent to ignore, Abraham sought to shift the blame.

The following were his excuses, briefly explained.

- Excuse #1: Look down on the religiosity (11a) of others. Abraham assumed that there was no fear of God in these people—perhaps because they were simply not his people. Yet, Abimelech and his court reacted in the fear of the Lord. We ought not promote immoral solutions merely because we look down on the religion of a group.
- Excuse #2: They are violent (11b). Abraham argued that he might be murdered so that others could take his wife. Even if the argument in granted that this particular region was known

for their violence, such does not justify immoral solutions and putting others in harm's way.
- Excuse #3: The technical argument . . . that misses the main point. Once again, Abraham argues that he and Sarah are relatives of some sort. While technically true, that is not the point, and his argument is an evasion. It is uncanny how quickly we may construct superficial arguments that miss the real point.
- Excuse #4: Blame the wife. Finally, he seeks to justify his actions by asserting that this was a prior agreement of a method by which Sarah would prove her love. Blame-shifting faults her instead of Abraham confessing and repenting.

Bruce Waltke deduces a general truism from this passage in his commentary: "The presentation of Abraham's weaknesses is significant to the picture of Abraham's character. The biblical heroes, God's covenant partners, are never superhuman; their great acts of faith are often bounded by failings and fears. Abraham clearly struggles with his own flawed patterns. The fears he confesses here actually distinguish his obedience and faith. At Abraham's great moments of faith and leadership, the narrator does not reveal his inner thoughts."[17] Waltke then continues to note specifically, "But the man presented in this scene must have overcome his fears as he left his homeland at God's command, as he risked war for brotherly commitment and justice, or as he dared to approach God to protect the righteous. Abraham has just demonstrated tremendous leadership, and he will soon faithfully obey God's most challenging command. By revealing Abraham's weaknesses in the midst of these significant events, the narrator captures the magnitude of Abraham's obedience and also inspires the readers' own faith struggles." This work agrees with Waltke's general thesis stated earlier in his commentary: "The disclosure of Abraham's failures also confirms God's sovereignty and power. He is gracious in election and capable of working out his good purposes through his human servants."

Abimelech may well have been more moral than Abraham in this case—a sad commentary on believers when we act out of pragmatism

---

[17] Bruce Waltke, *Genesis: A Commentary* (Zondervan, 2001), 284.

or cowardice. Abimelech honored Abraham (v. 14), even though wronged. He offered him land (v. 15). Irony and atonement gifts (v. 16) are provided. He informs Sarah that he is giving her "brother" the equivalent of a year's wages, along with livestock and human workers.

God blessed Abimelech, a non-Jewish person who obeyed God. And Abraham is a prophet who would pray (20:7) for him. Abimelech's wife and court were then healed of the inability to bear children. Abimelech knew that it was a great value to have this praying man of God in his community. He was happy to reward him for the religious benefit.

Moreover, the ruses and excuses were not necessary at all.

God would keep his promise. As the opening verses (1-7) of the next chapter show, the Isaac's birth comes about. Just as God had predicted, Sarah gave birth. And her son would always be called: "He Laughed." Her barrenness was cured in chapter 21. God keeps his promises—even when the participants in the covenant are less than perfect.

Later, the NT will affirm that if we are faithful, God will show his faithfulness (2 Tim. 2:13). But even if we are faithless, he will not deny himself.

Amidst scandal and slander, deceit and depravity, God is light and there is no darkness whatsoever in him (1 Jn. 1:5).

And surely, this ruse will never happen again. Or will it?

Fear and Trembling (Genesis 22)

Abraham has repeated his earlier mistake of seeking to protect himself by passing off Sarah as his sister a second time in Genesis 20. Also God gives to him and Sarah a precious child, Isaac. These parents had waited and waited and waited for this son. It would be tempting not only to cherish him but perhaps also to over-cherish him.

It's possible to idolize even the good gifts of God like children. In fact, any created thing can become wrongly valued and we may end up worshipping those cuddly, pink little "flesh covered idols" as Charles Spurgeon once called them. We might not have been that tempted to idolize our children—with such a busy and demanding pace when young—but most people agree that grandchildren can be more tempting.

Recall that God had given this promise to Abraham back as early as Genesis 12:3b when he called Abram from his home and promised to bless all nations through him. In the very next chapter, God told him that his offspring would be as countless as the grains of dust (13:15-16). The promise of a child is reiterated in Genesis 15:4-5 when God promises descendants as numberless as the stars in the sky. When God changes the patriarch's name from "exalted father" (Abram) to "father of multitudes" (Abraham), such cannot come about until the first descendant is born. God also confirmed his promise to bring a child about—incredulous as it may have seemed—through Abraham and Sarah (Gen. 18:13-15). Finally, the promise is delivered in Genesis 21 with the birth of the son named "He laughs."

Sarah had initially laughed (Gen. 18) when a messenger announced that she would give birth in her advanced age. God also told Abraham what to name the lad who would be born to Sarah. In a play on words (Gen. 21:5-7), these parents who are nearing the century-mark, name the child "Isaac," which means laughing lad. Sarah attempts to recover from her earlier doubting-laughter about God's promise, stating that all who see this miracle would join in laughing with her to rejoice over this birth. It is a birth that prepares us for a later virgin birth.

However, in between there is more family tension. Sarah instructs Abraham to get rid of Ishmael and Hagar. God joins Sarah in telling Abraham to get rid of his son, Ishmael. Abraham will have to be ready to lose both of his sons—even the promised one in chapter 22 of Genesis.

Yet, God still cares for the outcast Ishmael and Hagar, now a single mother. Rather than allowing Ishmael to wither and die, the Lord rescues the lad at the very last minute, pointing to an oasis and a well. Hagar re-fills the water skin and Ishmael lives in the wilderness, developing his archery skills and eventually marrying. The Lord is showing how he protects even those from imperfect home backgrounds.

The Friend of God at his Best

Having seen several prior lapses in Abraham's behavior, as we read these verses in this climactic narrative of Genesis 22, we nearly find ourselves waiting to see if Abraham fails. We almost expect him at any moment to negotiate with God or blame his wife or seek to misunderstand—which might have been plausible under the circumstances. Yet, he does none of those things. In fact, he rises to meet the challenges of this occasion.

Genesis 22 provides a peak performance as we see a parent who will give his most cherished child to the Lord.

Some years after Hagar and Ishmael are exiled, now God will test Abraham, calling on him to sacrifice his son, his only son (phrasing that will recur in the Gospel of John 1:18 and 3:16; also 1 John 4:9).

God calls Abraham to sacrifice that which is most valuable to him—his son, his only son (of promise). The Lord addresses Abraham, who reports for readiness ("Here I am.") and instructs Abraham to take his only son and travel to Moriah in order to sacrifice him there as a burnt offering. The Hebrew phrase that eventually led to the term "holocaust," is the root of the burnt sacrifice. Isaac was to be slain, totally incinerated on the altar. That call is clear—incomprehensible though it may be.

Abraham obeyed quickly; he prepared the donkey, chopped wood for the fire, enlisted two servants and began his three-day trek—agonizing at every mile and haunted by his thoughts at each step. The distance required 15-16 miles to be covered each of the three days. Surely, the nights afforded little more than fitful dreams. Nevertheless, Abraham obeyed.

When the party of four reached the mountain, Abraham ordered that his two servants remain behind, and they placed the wood on Isaac's back (v. 6). Isaac was a young teenager and capable of carrying a cord of wood. As such, he likely could have physically resisted his 100 year old father had he wished, but he did not.

Showing his faith, as Abraham left the servants, he instructed them to remain behind, while he and Isaac "will worship and then we will come back to you." (v. 5) The claim that "we" will come back seems, as many commentators have noted, to indicate that Abraham trusted God, somehow to preserve Isaac.

Every part of this narrative, if taken at face value, indicates that Abraham had only one intent, namely to obey God and sacrifice Isaac. Abraham had even brought the fire (or a flintstone to burn the sacrifice) and a sword large enough to slay the lad.

Isaac, then noted that something essential seemed to be missing. He asked his father where the sacrificial lamb was who would be sacrificed. Abraham answered that the Lord would provide for the burnt offering (v. 8). They continued toward the place of sacrifice. There Abraham constructed an altar, laying the wood underneath to burn it once slain. He also tied Isaac and proceeded to kill his son, his only son, whom he loved.

Many writers have speculated on what was going through Isaac's mind all this time. Furthermore, literature is filled with conjectures about Abraham's agonized thoughts. After waiting for over 25 years, after receiving repeated promises that the Lord would provide and give him a child of promise who would lead to universal blessings, now the one intersecting point that could thwart all that is about to be strangled. Moreover, how could a parent who knew the wrongness of murder kill his own child? Abraham was racked with doubts at every step, every hour, and especially at this moment.

The classic Rembrandt painting of this episode depicts the aged Abraham covering Isaac's mouth and raising his chin to be able to cut his throat. He is about to do this terrible deed—he is intent on sacrificing the most cherished thing in life. He wants nothing to come between him and the God of the covenant. Rembrandt even depicts the Angel of the Lord grabbing Abraham's arm before it descends to spill Isaac's blood.

The text simply says that an angel of the Lord called out doubly: "Abraham! Abraham!" The sacrifice was interrupted with the command not to sacrifice Isaac. Instead, the angel reports that God knows that Abraham fears God truly, "because you have not withheld from me your son, your only son." (v. 12)

Then the Lord directed Abraham's attention to a nearby thicket where a ram was ensnared by his horns. This animal is slain instead and then wholly incinerated or holocausted. Thus, Abraham named the place, "The Lord will provide."

God, then, reconfirms the covenant promise (22:15-18), telling Abraham that he will be blessed, his faith, has been proven, and his descendants will bless the entire world. Abraham returns to his servants (both he and Isaac as promised), and they travel back to Beersheba.

Lessons to Learn

Just as in chapter 18, God did not change his mind. All along he planned to rescue Isaac. But Abraham's faith was tested and he passed. God did not change, but Abraham learned a mighty lesson.

Also, this passage is a lasting lesson that we must be willing to follow God, even when at times it seems incomprehensible. No parent is asked to do this as Abraham was. Yet, we must be willing to give up all that we have to follow Christ (Jesus, in the Gospel of Matthew, instructs that we must, if need be, value Christ even over one's mother, father, brother, etc). In other words, we can let nothing interfere with following our God.

Nineteenth Century Danish philosopher Soren Kierkegaard was fascinated by this episode and thought it was a classic case for existentialism (also Calvin's disciple, Theodore Beza, wrote a play based on this). Kierkegaard argued in his 1843 *Fear and Trembling* that Abraham was torn and made a choice with real human freedom. Kierkegaard depicted Abraham as a "Knight of Faith," who resigned the most precious thing while at the same time taking a leap of faith. This faith must be, according to the Dane, personally chosen and based more on passion than duty (as Kant had earlier stressed).

While some of that may help us appreciate this episode in Genesis, Abraham also was not blindly making choices but choosing within the frame of God's speaking.

Finally, this drama that occurred two millennia before Jesus' own death has too many parallels to Christ's own sacrifice to ignore. While no human parent is asked to go through with this sacrifice, there was a Father who had a son, an only son whom he loved (John 1:18 and 3:16), and that Father did sacrifice his Son. He went through with it—whereas Abraham was spared. Instead of the wood under the altar, Jesus was sacrificed on a wooden cross-altar. The Father did not spare his own son (Rom. 8:32) but offered him up for us. Jesus the Son cried out in dereliction (Mt. 27:46) and agony, but the sacrifice still occurred.

The New Testament explains this great love as unique. While in the rarest of moments, one might give his life in exchange for another—and then it is only for one that we love or value (Rom. 5:6-8)—God sacrifices his only Son for us while we were not lovely but in fact were adversaries of God. What Wondrous Love is This!

Further, Hebrews 11:17-19 indicates that Abraham could act in faith because he knew that even if Isaac were slaughtered, God could raise him up again. Abraham acted in faith. Think of how this is represented in Genesis 22. In faith, Abraham:

- Traveled a distance of 45-50 miles to sacrifice his prized child.
- Prepared all that was needed for the sacrifice.
- Foretold that he and Isaac would return.
- Placed Isaac on the altar and drew his sword.
- Knew that the Lord would provide.
- Trusted that, if need be, God could raise Isaac from the dead.
- Did not withhold his only son but truly feared and honored God.

This was the supreme test, and Abraham passed it with flying colors. After years of following the Lord and obeying, the father of all faithful (see Rom. 4:16-25) did not waver in his faith. He did not seek excuses or attempt to counter-offer God's command. He was a champion of faith. Even though he'd had earlier lapses, this time, in fear and trembling (Phil. 2:12), this time, Abraham the friend of God (see also James 2:21-23) obeyed God and did exactly as the Lord commanded.

That, even when it calls for supreme sacrifice, is the way of faith.

How I Met Your Mother (Genesis 24)

The last verses in Genesis 22 shift the focus slightly away from Abraham's family to the descendants of Nahor, Abraham's brother. Those 12 sons are listed and connect to the line of Rebecca. The narrative is clearly heading toward the courtship of Isaac and Rebecca. First, however, chapter 23 will focus on the death and burial of a godly, female role model.

Mother Sarah: Death and Burial

Sarah lived to the age of 127—she is the only female whose long lifespan is recorded in the Bible. She enjoyed watching young Isaac grow into manhood for 37 years. Yet, after this long life, she dies and Abraham seeks an appropriate burial for her.

Human beings were buried from the earliest of times. It was an act of honor (and to avoid the shame of exposure and decomposition) to bury a person. And burial, contrary to many western customs, was not an act of lowering into the ground but of inserting into a cave.

Death is an expected reality of the OT, even though today many of us act as if our lives here will never end. God predicted in Gen. 2:17 that upon eating the forbidden fruit, death would ensue. Romans 5:12-17 echoes that same origin of human death. Genesis 5 continues that drumbeat genealogy, with each generation reported as: "and he died." To be sure, the wages of sin is death (Rom. 6:23), and it is designed that all people die, followed by judgment (Heb. 9:27). Job affirmed that if God did not provide breath we would surely die (Job 34:14-15); Proverbs 30:16 states that the grave is insatiable. David affirmed that our exact number of days are charted for us by the sovereign God (Ps. 139:16), and Moses spoke of the certainty of death and fleetingness of life (Ps. 90:3, 5-6, 10). The Lord himself not only expects cessation of human life, but the death of his saints is precious in his sight (Ps. 116:15).

Thus, the OT saints did not deceive themselves about the reality of death. Abraham sought to honor Sarah with an appropriate burial. And to do so, he negotiated to purchase the first real estate in Canaan. He was acting on the promise of God to give Abraham this land; thus, he wanted Sarah's body—and his other descendants—to be a memorial in that land. Although he was honored as a mighty prince, he had no standing or rights of citizenship in this land, controlled by the dominant Hittites.

Those Hittites respected him for his military victories (See Gen. 14) and his burgeoning estate. They even offered (three times in chapter 23) to give him a burial tract, but he insisted on purchasing a plot with a cave. In the end, he paid a costly price (400 shekels of silver; compared to the plot for the Temple in David's time, 2 Sam. 24:24), but he did so to ensure that Sarah's tomb would not be moved by future generations and that he would not be a debtor in this transaction. For once, Abraham was even out-negotiated by Ephron the Hittite.

However, Sarah was properly buried in the Cave of Machpelah, which has become a highly sacred memorial for Jews. Abraham intended that his covenant family would rest in the land promised by God. Others would also be buried here as well (see Gen. 49:29-32; 50:4-14; and Heb. 11:13-16). This was part of Sarah's final witness to God's faithfulness. The act of leaving her body in Canaan was central to the lasting witness of the patriarchs. John Calvin commented that while they themselves would one day be "silent, the sepulcher cried aloud, that death formed no obstacle to their entering on the possession" of Canaan. Later, another tomb also witnessed that God would triumph over human death.

Pre-Online Dating

Chapter 24 resumes, after this short description of the burial of Sarah, with God's provision of a wife for Isaac—the next generation of covenantal progress. The narrative in this chapter may be useful to illustrate what to look for in a spouse, and this is far from online dating. There are elements of romance, to be sure, in this, but also elements of practicality. It's somewhat amazing that such a beautiful love story is tucked amidst such weighty narratives.

Rebekah's family was introduced in Genesis 22:23. One of Nahor's sons is Bethuel, her father. This longest chapter in Genesis (twice as long as the chapter on creation) portrays Abraham as old and alone. He has one remaining large task, namely, to pass the covenantal baton to Isaac, which necessitated finding a wife. The scenes of this well-told story, which transfers patriarchal status, take place in 3 households: Abraham's (vss 1-9), Bethuel's (vss 28-60), and Isaac and Rebekah's (vss 66-67).

Abraham commissions his chief servant, likely Eliezer (cf. 15:2-3). He has this servant swear an oath to do just as he is instructed, at the risk of his life and limb—not to mention his reputation. The charge from Abraham is to find a wife for Isaac, but not from the neighboring Canaanites. The wise servant enquires about a possibility—exhibiting foresight and wisdom—should he find a wife but that she demands to stay in her land with her people. Abraham confirms that such would not be acceptable. Isaac's wife must be from his people and also must be willing to relocate to Abraham's estate. The servant agrees.

Off he journeys about 400 miles—let's call him "Eliezer"—with 10 camels and many other gifts. As he approaches a well in the vicinity of Abraham's distant family. Once he reaches that point, he prays a touching and pious prayer, asking the Lord to confirm the right woman for Isaac. She would be the one who (a) offers him a drink, and (b) also offers to water the flock of camels.

Out comes a beautiful, teenage virgin, who had not slept with a man. Rebekah is morally upright, works hard, comes from a strong family culture, shows care for others and resources, and she exhibit real faith, trusting in God (v. 58) to marry a man she'd never met.

And she satisfies the prayer request—a specific one—exactly. She offers Eliezer a drink and then proceeds to water his camels, which would have required many trips to the well and considerable time. She is welcoming to this outsider—a signature of hospitality.

Eliezer rejoices in praise, perhaps even scaring her a bit, and asks if he might stay in some guest quarters. She invited him to her home, noting that there was plenty of straw and fodder if this traveler needed to stay in a manger. Eliezer then showers her with gifts made of costly gold.

Once Eliezer arrives at the home of Bethuel (described as her mother's household, likely signaling that Bethuel has died since brother Laban does all the negotiation for this engagement), Laban comes out to greet him. We will see more of Laban's character later as he deals with Jacob, but already he is depicted as highly interested in the gold rings and bracelets that Eliezer has given to Rebekah. Or to put it this way: Laban might not have run out to welcome this visitor if he'd arrived on one donkey (instead of with 10 camels in tow) and plastic bracelets.

Eliezer asks to postpone the proposed welcome-feast so that he might first tend to business. He rehearses the whole story, beginning with Abraham's requirements (not a Canaanite wife, and not one who would take Isaac away), his journey, his prayer, and the obvious answer to that prayer by Rebekah's actions. He concludes by proposing on behalf of Isaac. Laban and the house of Bethuel (if Bethuel is gone, his wife represents him along with Laban in giving the blessing) agree to the proposal and the feast ensues.

This chief, trusted steward, is known for his good judgment (v. 5), his piety and prayer, his devotion to his employer, his faith that God will show himself and work through providence, and for his resolve to finish the drill. We see why Abraham depended on him so much. Eliezer has to be feeling pretty good about this mission.

The next day, Laban attempts to bargain for a ten-day delay, perhaps wishing to up the ante, but Eliezer is resolute that she must return with him that day. The family, then, brings her in and asks her if she'll move and marry Isaac, sight unseen. Some may view this as either an attempt of a teenager to get out on her own or as herself enamored by the wealth of her suitor, but it is also possible that God is teaching us that she had trust faith and trust in God.

Rebekah confirms that she wishes to travel and marry the servant's "lord," so they pack up her things, a servant-nurse, and it took the 10 camels to transport things back. Rebekah leaves Bethuel's home, and she rides many days in the desert on a camel. She had ample time to reconsider and return, but she does not.

When the party approaches Abraham's estate, Isaac sees the posse in the distance, but still has not laid eyes on Rebekah. As they draw nearer, she asks who that person in the distance is, and the servant informs her that that is Isaac. She liked what she saw, and veiled her face in modesty as she prepares to meet Isaac for the first time.

The servant did his job, God answered his prayer and led him, now Isaac takes Rebekah into his own dwelling and loved her and found comfort after the loss of Sarah, his mother.

Isn't this a great story?! While I don't recommend following every step of this chapter literally, it nevertheless is instructive of many principles for finding a spouse. Among those are:

- Look first for godly character and dependability.
- Look for a spouse from a believing family.
- Look for a spouse who believes in prayer and providence.
- Look for a spouse who will serve others, including showing care for resources (camels).
- Look for a spouse who will leave one's father and mother, cling to you, and become one flesh.

Rebakah's age and beauty were bonuses.

Isaac loved her immediately. It is truly love at first sight. And Abraham's servant is remembered for this superb mission.

Like a popular sitcom, we may have our own tales about "How I met your mother," and it will be hard to top this one. But each of us should learn to look to God's providence in identifying one's spouse. And it also helps to have good, reliable friends looking with you.

Abraham will soon pass away. Isaac and Rebekah are the next leaders. Although, only a few chapters are devoted to Isaac, he continues the covenant line, and Rebekah is mentioned once in the NT (Rom. 9:10). The Lord has drawn for us—even amidst the greed of brother Laban, the challenges of the day, and the odds of bringing home a total stranger for Isaac—how wonderful an institution marriage is and how it should be enjoyed. We may not know the physics behind what makes marriages work, but our love may grow from our faithfulness to one another, and we learn to thank God for his providence in leading us to wonderful spouses.

Marriage is a great rose of joy, even if depravity and sin surround.

The End of an Era; the Continuation of Some Things (Genesis 25-26)

Abraham's life is about over. His wife Sarah has died and has been buried. Prior to her death, he had taken another wife, Keturah (one Bible version says "took," but that is misleading, as if he only married Keturah in his 140s). In addition to the twelve sons given to Hagar (see Gen. 25:12-18), along with Keturah's six sons in the early verses of chapter 25, Abraham was the father of 20 sons. Each of those became tribes or nations. Abraham was, as God promised, the father of many nations.

These chapters seek to detail fully Abraham's family line. Of course, the line through Isaac is the most important, and it is taken up in Genesis 25:19-34. Prior to that, however, there is a touching and vivid description of Abraham's death. Twice in chapter 25 a phrase is used, namely, "gathered to his people." It is tempting to equate that with physical burial in the Cave of Macpelah. However, I will resist that temptation.

At Abraham's death, several descriptions are given. First, he was an old man of full age. True, he was 175 years old and that life-span is gradually declining from Noah's time. But one who lives a full life is one who has been blessed. Second, he is said to "breathe his last," indicating that even at this early time, cessation of respiration is a sign of mortality. These early saints understood that at human death the major anatomical systems ceased functioning; and the most telltale was the end of breathing. Thirdly, Abraham was "gathered to his people."

To be sure, verses 10-11 describe that his bones were deposited in the previously purchased cave where Sarah's body rested. "Gathered to his people" (v. 8) is also likely a hint of heaven—likely a poetic description of eternal life. As such, even these OT saints knew that there was eternal life, and that a social association was possible after our bodies are buried.

"Gathered to his people" is used 10 times in the OT, all in the Pentateuch (Gen. 25:8, 17; 35:29; 49:29, 33; Num 20:24, 26; 27:13; Dt. 32:50). Hamilton refers to this as a 4-fold process. "An individual breathes his last, dies, is gathered to his kin, and is buried. Dying precedes being gathered to one's kin, and being gathered to one's kin precedes burial. Therefore, to be gathered to one's kin cannot mean to be entombed in the grave. That one is gathered to one's kin/fathers before being buried implies either a belief in a continued existence" (168) or that there is some kind of family solidarity after physical death. Not all of the patriarchs who were "gathered to their kin were buried in an ancestral grave (i. e., Abraham, Ishmael, Moses, and Aaron).

Abraham (and later Ishmael in v. 17, even with his bad reputation at points) is gathered to his believing people in heaven. His bones are buried in a cave, but he continues his fellowship—as do believers in any century—after physical death with other saints (our people) in heaven.

Yet, his life has now ended. But it is a life to be remembered for generations. If you don't think Abraham was a giant of our faith, consider some of the many verses in the Bible that refer to him. The Book of Exodus refers to him often. Seven times the Book of Deuteronomy refers to him (1:8; 6:10; 9:5; 9:27, 29:134; 30:20; and 34:4)—and each time if specifies that Abraham "swore," emphasizing the covenant. 1 Chronicles records his entire family lineage in its opening chapter. Several Psalms refer to him also (47:9 and 105: 6, 9, 42), and the prophet Isaiah seemed especially interested in him (29:22; 41:8; 51:2, 63:16). Abraham is extolled throughout the OT.

Further, in the NT, he is mentioned at the outset in Matthew's genealogy, as he is in Mary's and Zechariah's songs (Luke 1:55, 73). Luke refers to Abraham as a historical figure in Luke 13:16 and 16:22-29. John summons him in his 8th chapter, concluding with Jesus' strong statement of deity that "Before Abraham was, I am"—and expression that any grammar teacher would mark off, unless it is understood that he is tying himself to the name of Jahweh. Abraham is mentioned in early church sermons—Acts 3:13 and extensively in Acts 7 (2, 8, 16, 32). Of course, Romans 4 draws on him heavily as does Galatians 3.

Abraham, though dead, still speaks, and according to Hebrews 11 his faith was characterized by looking forward to a city, but not one of earth. Abraham's faith propelled his vision to the city of God rather than to any earthly city, leading to identify as an alien in this world. And James calls him a "friend of God." (James 2:21, 23)

His faith is the same as ours. We owe him much and would do well to imitate his faith.

Yet, true faith goes on to the next generation of Abraham's children.

Isaac the Successor

Isaac's line is introduced in the second half of Genesis 25. Ishmael's 12 tribes are also recorded compactly as a unique cycle. It is worth noting that God does not cast Hagar's descendants aside. In fact, immediately after the record of Abraham's death is the "toledoth" (line of descendants) of Ishmael in Gen. 25:12-18. Below is a review of how the book of Genesis is organized around this conceptual idea.

Below is an outline of Genesis, based on a key Hebrew phrase (*toledoth*) used 10 times.

	Gen. 1:1-2:3	The origins of the cosmos
•	Tablet 1: Gen. 2:4-4:26	The origins of mankind
•	Tablet 2: Gen. 5:1-6:8	The history/cycle of Adam's line
•	Tablet 3: Gen. 6:9-9:29	The history/cycle of Noah
•	Tablet 4: Gen. 10:1-11:9	The history/cycle of Noah's sons
•	Tablet 5: Gen. 11:10-11:26	The history/cycle of Shem
•	Tablet 6: Gen. 11:27-25:11 Abraham	The history/cycle Terah &
•	Tablet 7: Gen. 25:12-25:18	The history/cycle of Ishmael's line
•	Tablet 8: Gen. 25:19-35:29	The history/cycle of Isaac's line
•	Tablet 9: Gen. 36:1-36:43	The history/cycle of Esau
•	Tablet 10: Gen. 37:1-50:26	The history/cycle of Jacob's sons

The seventh tablet or cycle is Ishmael's; and God kept his promises to this outlier. Even though they were constantly in conflict with their neighbors, still the Lord keeps his promise to Hagar and Ishmael.

Abraham enjoyed Isaac for 40 years (and the twin grandsons for 15 years) before the patriarch passed away. Isaac was happily married to Rebekah, the sister of Laban. For a season, Rebekah (like Isaac's mother, Sarah) was barren, and Isaac prayed for her. It took 20 years for this birth-prayer to be answered, but when Isaiah was 60 (25:26), the Lord answered this prayer—surely a lesson in persevering in prayer. Eventually, she conceived twins, and those two lads wrestled within her, leading her to ask God why this was happening.

The Lord explained to Rebekah that there were two proto-nations in her womb, and that in a very unusual turn, the older would serve the younger. Normally, in Hebrew families, the oldest child was considered superior, but it would not be so in this case. When she delivered these fraternal twins, the first to be born was Esau, named after his hairy appearance (later, his reddish skin tone was associated with Edom, which means red). Shortly thereafter, his younger brother, Jacob, was born—clutching the heel of Esau. The word "Jacob" means "grasper"—and this would be a clue to his character.

The first episode about these lads (25:27-34) illustrates their character in vivid hues. Esau was an outdoorsman—he would have watched ESPN or the hunting channel—and his father loved him. Jacob was more of a home-body—a subscriber to HGTV—and Rebekah preferred him. One day after hunting (likely for no more than 6 hours), Esau returned, and smelled a great stew that Jacob was cooking. Esau claimed to have been famished (surely, hyperbole), and he demanded some of Jacob's stew.

Jacob bargained back, asking for Esau first to sell his birthright for a helping of chili. Esau revealed his short-sightedness and desire for immediate gratification, saying: "Look, I'm about to die. What good is the birthright to me?" This was sinful on many levels—easily observed.

Jacob made the older brother swear an oath to transfer the birthright (v. 33; this was clearly premeditated and exploitative), and then gave him some deluxe stew. Jacob, the grasper, won the negotiation hands down. The chapter concludes by noting that Esau despised his birthright.

The Lord will use Jacob, and the third quarter of the Book of Genesis will show much deception and scandal from these scoundrels.

Still, the march of God's sovereign salvation will march on—even through these defective twins and this imperfect family.

Wife-Deceit (Genesis 26:1-34): Third Strike and You're Out (cf. Gen. 12b, 20)

Before we move forward with those twins, though, Genesis 26 depicts a third time the old "Pass your wife off as your sister to save yourself" tactic is used—this time by the generation after Abraham.

A famine comes to the land (26:1; note, the reference to a different one in Abraham's time precludes the author thinking this was a one-time event that clumsy editors jumbled), and Isaac seeks to provide for his family by relocating to Gerar. The chapter has three scenes:

a. 26:1-16 At Gerar
b. 26:17-22 At the Wadi of Gerar
c. 26:23-33 At Beersheba

In the first scene, God renews his covenant with Isaac along the same lines as he did with Abraham. In the second scene, there are quarrels over limited natural resources—leading to a division of the territory. In the third scene, Abimelech sues for a non-aggression pact with Isaac because God is so manifestly blessing the patriarch.

Bruce Waltke (loc cit) shows the parallels of form between Abraham and Isaac.

ABRAHAM
A. 12:1-3 Receives God's call and promise
B. 12:10-20 Wife-sister deception episode
C. 13:1-12 Quarrel with Lot's men; Abraham takes lesser land
D. 15:1-21 Divine reassurance and a sacrifice
E. 21:22-24 Treaty with Abimelech at Beersheba

ISAAC
- A. 26:2-6   Receives God's call and promise from God
- B. 26:7-11   Wife-sister deception episode
- C. 26:14-22 Quarrel with Abimelech's men and other local men; Isaac moves rather than fight
- D. 26:23-25 Divine reassurance and a sacrifice
- E. 26:26-33 Treaty with Abimelech at Beersheba

Throughout this passage, Isaac interacts with Abimelech.[18] Although this is the same name as in Genesis 20, it is likely a royal title—it means "my father was king," thus used for a prince enroute to the throne—since the span of years is large. Nevertheless, Isaac seeks to pass his wife off as his sister (this must have been prior to the birth of the twins). He expected her to catch the king's eye, but did not want to risk his own life.

Abimelech is more moral than most rulers of the day. He clearly understood that there were consequences for adultery and did not wish to violate another man's wife. When he sees Isaac and Rebekah being more friendly than siblings, he sees through the ruse and confronts Isaac. Isaac admits his error. Ultimately, Abimelech asks for a treaty with Isaac because he believes that God is with the son of Abraham.

Was Abimelech a believer? It is possible; it is also possible that he was only conforming to minimal religious standards from self-interest. This Abimelech, though, was discerning; he did honor the sanctity of marriage and accepted that adultery had ethical ramifications; he did acknowledge Isaac's God; and he did desire to be on the right side of God's Spirit. It is also the case that he may have made a confession out of self-interest.

Notwithstanding, if we compare his confession with several others from the OT, we are confirmed in seeing that God works in much more than a single nation. Consider the fine theology seen in these non-Hebrew confessions in the OT:

---

[18] Abimelech was a royal name. Cf. superscription of Ps. 34, while 1 Sam. 21:10-15 identifies the king as Achish. Rather than questioning the accuracy of an admittedly strange narrative, it is helpful to see that there are many "Abimelech" characters in Scripture, normally a royal title not so much a surname.

- Jethro (Ex. 18:10-11). Note the sturdy grasp and theology in his remarks.
- Rahab (Josh. 2:9-11). Note the praise and insight of a non-Hebrew who will be included in the genealogy of Jesus.
- Namaan (2 Kings 5:15). Note, even if a tad self-interested.

God can bring to himself all kinds of people. Those he draws to himself are not already perfect, nor do they attain moral greatness prior to the Spirit working in them. He can draw scoundrels, pagan rulers, shifty ("grasper") brothers, harlots, and even the socially upright to himself. Such is his sovereign salvation.

Thankfully, this will be the last recorded time that a patriarch seeks to pass off his wife as his sister. One may look condescendingly on this repeated subterfuge, but we might also be a bit cautious in thinking that we are morally superior. Times were tough, and one could lose his head in a hurry. Even though this was deceptive, God still used Isaac.

And if one thinks the deception and depravity is clear in chapter 26, wait until that is further chronicled in the next chapter. There is, I agree, a literary contrast between Isaac, who is the deceiver (ch. 26) but the deceived in ch. 27. "The villain becomes a victim, and a nemesis is at work in his life as much as it is in the life of his younger son." (Hamilton, 190)

The Deceiver Grasps; Whole Lotta Deceit and Dysfunction: Jacob and Esau (Genesis 27)

In this chapter, I want to count the number of deceptions, parenting failures, and absences of faith. I do so, not rejoicing at others' weaknesses but believing that these chapters are recorded for us in order to provide a manual for what not to do.

We have already seen how Esau devalued his birthright and sold it for a bowl of stew. We've also seen Isaac seek to pass off his wife as his sister. Still, amidst all this, God is still working with this family and will continue to do so. This cycle also encourages all who do not have perfect families.

How Do I Deceive Thee, Let me Count the Ways

Chapter 27 of Genesis could be a textbook in family dysfunction, deceit, and spiritual decline.

Somehow, God uses all these things and all these characters. The deception is detailed, artistic, and almost Shakespearian in its tragedy. Isaac was over a 100 years of age. He would live at least another 40 years after this (Gen. 25:26; 26:34; 35:28). To be sure, he may have been frail, blind, and could have had a serious malady at the time. However, he lived on and there's no record of him ever reversing course.

It's an exercise to count the various instances of deceit in these verses. I list ten below.

1. Isaac sought to reverse the blessing that God revealed in 27:4 (cf 25:23). Even though he is old and fading, he makes a request of Esau. He asks his outdoorsman son to take his

hunting tools and kill some game and cook it the way he likes it. Isaac knew that God had ordained Jacob, not Esau, to receive his blessing. However, Issac acted exactly opposite of what God had said. The patriarch sought to alter God's blessing, seeking to reverse it.

2. Eve's-Dropping (27:5). Rebekah, however, does not trust Isaac. She is listening and eavesdropping (but the play on words to remind us of Eve's disobedience is in order). As soon as she hears Isaac's plan to give his blessing to Esau, following a great meal, she springs into action. Perhaps she had thought of this before, or else she rapidly connives. Whichever, she snoops, hears, and acts to reverse her husband's directive to Esau. To be sure, she may have had reasons to distrust Isaac, but this is a marriage filled with dysfunction and deceit.

3. Rebekah sought to grasp the blessing (27:10), even if dishonestly. Rebekah has a fully formed plan. She instructs Jacob to fetch and kill two goats and bring them back to her to be cooked in a special recipe. Like Jacob's name ('grasper'), she is grasping at a destiny that God has ordered but may be using methods that are far from normative.

4. Jacob initially objects to trickery (27:12). Rebekah's plan is so obviously a subterfuge that Jacob immediately feels uncomfortable with carrying it out. He objects that such is dishonest and his father will surely know. It is trickery to be sure.

5. Rebekah assumes too much responsibility (27:15). Rebekah does not want to hear Jacob's protest over ethical fine points. She tells him to do what she's said, and even promises to bear any responsibility. This is, some have noted, the first time in the pages of the OT when one person volunteers vicariously to take another's punishment. But it must be noted that she assumes more responsibility than she should.

6. Rebekah actively disguises Jacob (27:15-16). Next, she covers all her bases and anticipates Isaac's possible inspections. She instructs Jacob to get some of Esau's clothing, and then she

applies the long silky hair of a 'camel' goat to Jacob's arms and necks. She thoroughly thinks through this deceit. It's almost as if she has an entire makeup department for a stageplay at her ready disposal. And give her credit: she thought through all that was needed. Only Jacob's voice might give him away.

7. Jacob deceives about his identity (25:19). When Jacob first presents this amazing meal to his father, Isaac asks him who he is. Jacob lies. He is not fully involved in the deception. Isaac is a bit suspicious, but does not halt the action.

8. Jacob falsely reports certain facts (27:20). Isaac wonders how it is possible to have acquired the game and to have cooked it so quickly. It is suspicious, but it has the smell and appearance of the meal he requested. Isaac wanted the blessing-reversal so badly that he shelved discernment. And Jacob participates in the dishonesty.

9. Isaac asks again about identity (27:24), is lied to, but does not verify. As this drama approaches its climax, Isaac feebly inspects things, and even feels the hairy limbs of Jacob (credit Rebekah) and detects Esau's clothes (credit Rebekah again).

10. Isaac deceives himself. He thinks that he may act contrary to God's will and finds out that one cannot fool God.

The Blessing and Curse are quickly issued (27:27-29). Jacob is promised prosperity, irrigation for his crops, and that he will rule over his brothers. The deed is done. The man's word binds, even if self-deceived and deceived by others.

And this is exactly the blessing that God ordered and predicted. Despite all this deceit, dishonesty, and dysfunction, God's will is done. It will not be thwarted.

It's hard to find a hero in this. Isaac was in steep decline and did not show obedience to God. Jacob was happy to grasp at his older brother's blessing. Esau had already disrespected his birthright. And Rebekah is a quintessential conniver.

Perhaps she felt it was necessary to do whatever it took to carry out God's revealed promise of blessing. If so, she could be credited with faithfulness, even though her methods were not commendable.

It is not necessarily a feminist interpretation but a realist one to observe how Rebekah watched Isaac's continued spiritual lethargy and decline. And Esau was pretty disappointing. Perhaps, she stepped in to seek to conform to God's revelation that "the older would serve the younger." Yes, she used deceit and trickery; yes, she was usurping the husband's place. However, she also was implementing what God had revealed.

Isaac was not doing that.

The older Brother comes in shortly after the blessing has been irrevocably bestowed (27:30-40). Isaac is shocked, Esau is distraught, and the older brother tries to reverse both the given blessing and the promise of God. He begs Isaac to "think outside the box" and expand the options for blessing. Esau begs a panicked father to give him another blessing. Isaac does, but the blessing ends up not being a blessing.

This is drama at its best—a tragedy, really.

But God is working all his will out, even with such flawed characters. We would be wise to avoid many of these deceptive tactics. But we should also be wise enough to see that when God makes a promise—even if it reverses social customs, like blessings for the first born—it will and should come about.

The Deceiver/Conniver Realizes his Need for God (Genesis 28-29)

The final verses of Genesis 27 set the stage for new chapters in Jacob's life. This heir of the covenant is the most prominent character for about 20% of the book of Genesis.

After this stunning deception, Esau is ready to kill his brother. Esau planned to wait until his father, Isaac, died and then kill Jacob (27:41). Rebekah again intervenes to send Jacob away (27:42). She advises him to flee immediately to Haran to seek refuge with her brother Laban. He is to stay there until Esau's anger receded. She would signal him when his anger had subsided (27:45). Her recorded stream-of-consciousness motive was that she did not want to lose both sons in one day.

Rebekah then expressed extreme disgust (27:46) with the unbelieving women around her and her sons. She did not want Jacob to take an unbeliever to be his wife—a standard that is wise in all ages. Isaac, then, exhorted Jacob not to take a Canaanite woman as his wife (28:1) and sent him on his way with his blessing and the instruction to marry someone from his extended family in Laban's household. Isaac finally gets it right and speaks the blessing to Jacob, asking that God would bless him with fruitfulness, growth, and that he would possess the land.

After Jacob exits and heads to Laban's house (about 400 miles away; so out of range of daily revenge efforts), Esau learns that Isaac had renewed his blessing and counseled Jacob to marry a believer from a known family. It then dawned on Esau how revolting his marriages were to unbelievers. Esau may have read the handwriting on the wall and realized how grievous it was to his parents that he was married to

Hittite women. Thus, perhaps he tried to ingratiate himself to them by marrying a daughter of Ishmael.

Jacob then travels a lengthy distance, is on his own—away from his parents' influence—and meets God. As he travels, he finds a resting place, using a stone for a crude pillow. As he sleeps, God appears to him in a dream. The central object in the dream is a stairway (the old spiritual song depicts this as a ladder). Such 'mount' (one translation of the Hebrew word) was typically used to approach a walled city, with a flat side against the wall and a series of stairs on the opposite side facing away from the walled city that allowed an army to crest the wall and conquer.

Earlier, in Genesis 11, human beings also sought to create a tower that reached into the heavens. The stairway in Jacob's dream, however, was the result of God's condescension, not human beings seeking to storm heaven. And on this stairway were "the angels of God, ascending and descending." These exact words recur in John 1 as Jesus is calling his disciples. Those Jewish lads would immediately associate Jacob's ladder with its fulfillment in Jesus himself.

So impressive is this dream that Jacob praises God, recognizing this to be the 'house of God,' and the gateway to heaven.

Jacob dreamed of a ladder connecting earth and heaven. Prior to references to the Tabernacle, the sole occurrence of this phrase, "house of God," is in Genesis 28. In this dream, Jacob sees angels traversing up and down on this ladder. As confusing as this dream might seem (until Jesus explains it in John 1), Jacob deduces that this is a very special place, to be marked with a monument. Of this place, he says, "This is none other than the house of God. This is the gate of heaven."

He designated the name for this place as *Beth-el* (house of God). Then he solemnly promises that if God will be with me, and "will keep me in this way that I go, and will give me bread to eat and clothing to wear, so that I come again to my father's house in peace, then the Lord shall be my God, and this stone, which I have set up for a pillar, shall be God's house, and of all that you give me, I will give a tenth."

The repetition of the name ("house of God") has a purpose. Yet, there is no frame, no building, not even a tent. So how can this be God's *house*. T. David Gordon summarizes that the initial use of this expression (used three times here), "is not only not a building, it takes place in a mere dream of a world better than this. Somebody weighed down with the weight of his sin and that of others, his mortality and that of others, bereft of the blessedness of God's presence, has a dream that says maybe these two arenas will be bridged. 'In earth and heaven be one,' to use the language of the hymn, right? And just dreaming about it is thrilling to him. And so he calls it the house of God thrice, because the house of God is not a material thing that contains the triune God."[19]

So what did Jacob see? Jesus picks up this language verbatim in John 1, when he is calling the earliest disciples. When Jesus reveals his omniscience to Nathanael, he is amazed. Jesus responds by going one further: "You will see the angels of God ascending and descending on the Son of Man." Did you see how Christ ties that all together. He takes Jacob's dream and interprets himself as the connecting ladder with angels ascending and descending on him. Jesus assumed that those steeped in Jewish tradition and literature would make this association.

Dr. Gordon concludes: "What was done in Genesis 11 [Tower of Babel] was not permissible, namely, our getting back into the presence of God on our measure and manner is not permitted, but God gave Jacob his dream, and He gives the Israelites and us this picture that it's right for you to hope to be in the presence of God again, to dwell with God, to be in the house of God, and not to be left out and bereft of His presence." Even a rascal like Jacob can be redeemed, used, and point us to the Son of Man, who truly connects heaven and earth, with angels ascending and descending on him. Indeed, that is a dream to record and a place to mark.

God provides a house to meet with his people. The house of God is "not just the place where he resides; it's the place where he is met, and that's why it's called the tent of meeting." One day, the dwelling place of God will be with us; his presence will not be limited by a house. Already, the Eternal Word has become flesh and tabernacled among us.

---

[19] Taken from T David Gordon, "Biblical Theology and the 'House of Prayer'" in *On Reforming Worship* (Covenant Foundation, 2018).

Jacob, of course, could not possibly know all this. But this early occurrence in this dream displays both the unity of Scripture, as well as the organic nature of God's plan of salvation. He reveals in a dream—centuries before Jesus came—that a Mediator was needed between heaven and earth. That Mediator (Jacob's Ladder) was surrounded by angelic supervisors to make sure God's plan came about.

David Gordon concludes: "So yes, we meet God insofar as he can be met, and he is now reconciled by the work of his Son, and we are called his house, dignified by being called that. But entering there is not magical, and doesn't suddenly take people who love God most of the time and are indifferent about him other times, and so forth, and outright at war with him at others, it doesn't relieve all of that spiritual reality and warfare that's part of this life. But it is where God can be met by yet present, imperfect sinners. Right? That's where he is to be met."

God's promises made to Abraham are now reiterated to Jacob (13b-15). And Jacob may have come to faith for the first time. Note his believing reactions (16 ff):

a. His praise (vss 16-17). God is awesome, holy, and opens heaven to us.
b. His altar (vss18-19). Worship is a suitable response for true belief.
c. His vow (vss 20-21). Jacob promises to follow God.

His life is changed. Despite any defects in his past, he moves forward in a life of obedience to God.

Romance

400 miles later . . . and many hours in the weight room later (Jacob is transformed from an indoor cook to a super-human strongman), Jacob goes to Haran, as Rebekah had instructed. He discovers a well,[20] whose mouth is covered by a very large stone—think of the stone that was rolled across the tomb of Jesus—and such would normally require

---

[20] Note how many wells and watering daughters are repeated: Gen. 24, Gen 29, Exodus 2.

many men to move it. At that well, Jacob will meet Rachel—his distant cousin and fiancé.

When Jacob reaches this resting point, he asks if anyone knows Uncle Laban, who was Nahor's grandson (Nahor and Abraham were brothers). The herdsmen reply that they do, and Jacob inquires as to Laban's health. Then, in high romantic drama, Rachel shows up at the well. No one can water the 3 flocks until the massive stone is moved, and Jacob is transformed from sous chef to Superman. He singlehandedly moves the stone, the flocks can now be watered, and Jacob immediately embraces Rachel and weeps. His mother's prophecy is being fulfilled, and he thinks that he will soon have a wife, return home, and build a family.

He meets his father-in-law, Laban, who is also thrilled, and the romance is off to the races.

Jacob is converted, the possessor of Isaac's blessing, he has left his sketchy past behind, and he now has found a woman he loves and wishes to marry.

It appears that the conniver-in-chief is now on an uninterrupted path to good times.

Until he is out-connived.

The Conniver Out-Connived (Genesis 29b-30)

Laban was already introduced back in chapter 24. He is the older brother of Rebekah and the male leader of his household at that time. He is also lured by the bling of gifts that Abraham sent to entice Rebekah to come back to marry Isaac. In these chapters, we see even more details of his sneaky character.

He was thrilled at the suitor (Jacob) for his daughter Rachel. But Laban was never above conniving on his own and taking advantage of a situation.

This section of Genesis reveals jealousy, barrenness, marital dysfunction, deceit, and exploitative relatives. Below are observations from the conniver being connived. The irony is palpable.

Laban's initially offered to compensate Jacob for his work (29:15), saying that he did not wish to take advantage of him merely because they were relatives. Jacob offered to pay the bride price amounting to seven years of labor for Rachel. Laban smiled all the way to the bank.

Laban's daughters are introduced together in vss 16-17. Leah's name ("cow"), symbolized a large value but would have been hard to live down. Leah's eyes were delicate, either signifying understated beauty or visual impairment. Rachel's name ("ewe") might have been a bit easier to live up to. Verse 18 reiterates |Jacob's affection for Rachel and reports his agreement with Laban to work those seven years to win her hand (and to replace the lost productivity over the balance of her life to dad. To Jacob, that seven-year period flew by, and seemed like a mere span of days. Yes, love endures.

When the seven years are up, Jacob asks for the wedding to take place. He has paid all that he promised. Laban throws a drinking-festival—actually, it would be a week-long bridal party. Many friends and family were invited; all expected a long-awaited wedding between Jacob and Rachel.

Laban, however, did not keep his word. He played an unconscionably dastardly trick on Jacob, in which there was a disguised *reversal of an older for a younger sibling.* Laban cruelly substituted Leah, the older sister, for Rachel, the younger sister that Jacob loved so dearly and desired to marry.

Jacob and Leah had sex, and the next morning when Jacob awoke, as one older translation put it to stress the shock, "Behold! Leah." It is hard to explain how this all transpired.

Questions arise such as:

- Where was Rachel? What was she expecting? How did she not cling to Jacob?
- Where was Laban's wife? If she were alive, did she have nothing to say?
- Was Leah in on all of this? Was she cooperating with a partial parent to deceive, as Jacob did with Rebekah?
- Even if dark, with the presence of a veil, and great drunkenness, how incapacitated would Jacob have to have been not to realize that this was a ruse and deceitful substitution?

How can we explain this discovery? Several attempts are made, such as:

a. Drunkenness. Jacob would learn this lesson the hard way, if that is the explanation. Laban also would be complicit.

b. It was really dark, plus a bridal veil cloaked, but would not some sense of touch reveal the trick?

c. Patriarchical prerogative. Some attempt to justify Laban by a cultural custom. In fact, in v. 26, Laban's rationalization is based on the "custom" of marrying the oldest before the youngest.

Rachel, apparently, is left out of this. Later, Lev. 18:18 prohibits marrying sisters. This episode shows, "it is also an example of honest reporting, not reading back the law into an earlier time." (Kidner, 161)

Jacob perseveres and keeps his word and serves his time. He serves another seven years to win Rachel. Certainly, this is unfair, but we also see growing character in Jacob.

Jacob's family is then detailed, beginning in vss 31-35.

a. The Lord enables Leah alone (29:31-35) to have four children. Their names indicate how she sought the affection of Jacob and how her misery had been noted by God. She hopes that Jacob's love that was once reserved for Rachel would migrate to her. The score at the end of chapter 30 is: Leah 4, Rachel 0.

b. Rachel and Leah struggle for children via Bilhah and Zilpah (30:1-13) for four more children. Rachel is extremely jealous and demands to start her family by hook or crook. She willingly lends her handmaid Bilhah to be a surrogate mother with Jacob. Leah will so similarly. Verses 3-13 describe the following surrogate births.

- Bilhah → Dan (v. 6)
- Bilhah → Naphtali (v. 8)
- Zilpah → Gad (v. 11)
- Zilpah → Asher (v. 13). To round out the family line:
- Leah → Issachar (v. 18)
- Leah → Zebulun (v. 20)
- Leah → Dinah (v. 21)

The score is: Leah 6 sons, 1 daughter; Bilhah 2 sons, Zilpah 2 sons . . . Rachel 0.

Meanwhile, the "deceiver Jacob was deceived, and the despised Leah was exalted to become the mother of, among others, the priestly and kingly tribes of Levi and Judah." (Kidner, 160)

In between, there is another lurid episode, as Leah and Rachel struggle over mandrakes Vss. 14-17 chronicle an interlude about buying and selling paternity . Jealousy again rears its head! Rachel is so desperate to have children that she rents Jacob out. Leah's son, Reuben, comes home with a bundle of mandrakes, which were thought to be aphrodisiacs. Rachel wants some thinking that such will enable her fertility. Leah accuses her of first stealing her husband, Jacob, and then wanting to steal these "love apples," as one translation styles it.

Rachel will not admit to thievery, so she trades a night with Jacob to Leah. Jacob goes along with this, and other children are born to Leah. This is the 4th exchange in the Jacob *toledoth*: (1) exchange of birthright, (2) exchange of blessing, (3) exchange of wives, and (4) exchange of husband for sex-procreation.

Leah's womb is super productive, but she cannot gain what she wants—the love of Jacob. Rachel, on the other hand, had Jacob's affection, but could not produce any sons to continue his line.

Finally, Joseph a son is born (vss. 22-24to Rachel (Jacob's 11th son). And. this son will be crucial in leading to the line of Messiah Jesus.

Meanwhile, Laban has out-connived the conniver. Leah has many sons but not martial joy. Rachel is desperate, stooping to any depths to get a family. Jacob is growing into an admirable man who sticks to his word. And God is working, even amidst all this deceit, dysfunction, and depravity

This is why we sing Psalm 46:11: "The Lord Almighty is with us; the God of *Jacob* is our fortress."

The Out-Conniver Out-Connived (by both Jacob and Rachel) (Gen. 30:25-31:21)

Critics of the Bible love this section of Scripture. They often use it to attack the veracity of Scripture, contending that what Jacob did to engineer the herds of Laban is simply at odds with genetics. Nevertheless, we have a section in God's Word that also shows how trickery seems to escalate.

Could a mom say:

- "Stop making that face or your face will freeze"?
- "Put your tooth under your pillow, and the tooth fairy will reward you"?
- "Nothing good happens after midnight"?

Simply because a mother says such, does that make those ideas true? Or could it be that merely the report of the words/ideas spoken by a mom which are useful but not totally accurate? It may be that Jacob (and others in his day) believed that livestock DNA could be altered by visual fixation during conception. Then, again, whether that is true of not, this episode does not depend on any changing ideas of genetics. Instead, it is clear that this is a highly unusual event—likely unrepeatable—but one in which God provides over several layers of deceit and conniving.

Recall about this major familial deception:

    a.   Jacob was named for "grasping" what was not his. He was, along with his mom, a conniver.

    b.   Later, Jacob was out-connived by his father-in-law, Laban (with the old fiancé exchange).

    c.   Can Laban be out-connived?

Genesis 30:25ff. depicts the contract for the flocks and the contest between the schemers. In vss. 25-26, Jacob states that the full payment of his covenant is satisfied. He has paid his debt in full and wishes to return to his family. During this conversation, Laban's faith is shown to be wanting, characterized by: divination (v. 28; also 31:19), opportunism, and also flattery.

Jacob, however, has a truer sense of causation (29-30). He knows that God is at work amidst all of these acts that are not to be imitated.

Episode of Trickery

Jacob proposed that he receive a small portion of Laban's flocks—and the fraction was also, on the surface, to be made out of the weakest offspring. Laban was to keep all the solid-colored sheep, and Jacob would only take those that were mottled. This was, lest we become distracted by liberal criticism, a special case (Gen. 31:9-10).[21]

Laban agrees (v. 34) to this method, and thinks he has won another negotiation. However, this is little more than continued trickery and exploitation (35-36) on his part, as he seeks to remove even the stock that would lead to another generation of livestock.

Vss 37-42 detail Jacob's manipulation.[22] Through it all, Jacob receives God's blessing (v. 43).

It is important to glean what we can about God from this. In this colorful episode, we must observe, at least, the following traits or attributes of God.

    a. His sovereignty
    b. His justice
    c. His omniscience (31:12)
    d. His covenant faithfulness (31:13)

---

[21] If one wishes to review explanations of this, see: https://answersingenesis.org/genetics/animal-genetics/jacobs-odd-breeding-program-genesis-30/; or https://creation.com/jacobs-sheep.

[22] On v. 41, one commentator notes that "vigorous animals are hybrids whose recessive coloring genes emerge when they are bred together. Jacob can distinguish the stronger animals with the recessive gene by their copulating earlier than the weaker animals without that gene." Cited in Waltke, 420.

God is was work in his covenant family, even those fraught with deceit and depravity, exploitation or envy.

This is followed in the next chapter with Jacob's escape and more trickery. Note, the similarity of sequence to Gen. 28 in the outline below.

> 1-3 Another Great Escape
> 4-9 Jacob's plan
> 10-13 Another Dream; Covenantal assurance
> 17-21 The Flight, and a deception by Rachel

A chapter of Jacob's life, which began with an "ignominious departure from home," is closing. That chapter started with his own "effrontery in tricking both his father and his brother." (Baldwin, 127) That led to his flight, which led to a two-decade separation from his family. During that long and trying season, he may have wondered if he imagined the dream at Bethel. Thankfully, there was a stone memorial to that. Now, he is about to embark on another flight, following another dream, surrounded by layers of deceit and trickery. But he is also assured by the God of Bethel.

****

Appendix A: Below and referenced is an extract of an attempt to harmonize Genesis 31 with Genetics.
Science & Christian Belief, Vol 13, No. 1 (2001), 51–58
J. D. PEARSON
A Mendelian Interpretation of Jacob's Sheep

The story of Jacob producing flocks of striped goats and black sheep starting from flocks in which these characteristics had been removed is considered from a Mendelian genetic viewpoint. Previous commentators have implied that the placing of branches in front of the animals arose from the belief that vivid sights during pregnancy would leave a mark on the offspring. However, the fact that Laban removed all the coloured animals from the flock he entrusted to Jacob, shows that the herdsmen knew that the colour of the offspring was influenced in some way by the colour of the parents. It was not necessary for the herdsmen to understand the exact rules of inheritance, only sufficient that, wherever possible, female animals were served by coloured males. It is proposed that the use of the branches referred to in the story was not an attempt to generate visual impressions influencing the females during pregnancy or conception, but instead the branches were used to build a fence to ensure that only male animals could serve the females.

This paper takes the story at face value, and the principles of Mendelian genetics are applied to show how quickly the colour of the flock could have been changed by an experienced shepherd. After fourteen years of working with sheep, Jacob must have understood the importance of using rams with the desired characteristics to pass on these characteristics to some of the lambs. It is shown below that with the assumptions given, the colour of the animals could be changed into the form desired by Jacob over the period of six years. Complicating the model presented may amend the figures quoted but would not invalidate the conclusions.

Conclusions

It has been shown that contained in the sheep left by Laban in Jacob's keeping were sufficient recessive black genes to produce enough black rams to undertake a selective breeding programme. It is unnecessary to assume that such a procedure is a modern innovation. It has been shown that such a programme would produce a flock of predominantly black animals in a period of five years. In the period of six years in which the flock was in Jacob's keeping, Jacob would acquire most of Laban's flock. The biblical account emphasizes that the significance of the tree branches was at the actual mating, rather than during the pregnancies. There is strong evidence that both Laban and Jacob had knowledge of the importance of inherited characteristics. The breeding programme would have involved the isolation of the white rams. This could be achieved by constructing a wooden pen, and the construction of this pen can be inferred from the biblical account.

****

Focus OFF the Family (Genesis 31b-32)

Sometimes in a highly secularized society, we seek refuge in creations other than God for refuge or salvation. The family, an extremely blessed creation of God, can be, at times, one of those. In the 1980s, reeling from a variety of onslaughts against the traditional family, Dr. James Dobson came to prominence with his "Focus on the Family" ministry. He brought much common sense to matters and sought to strengthen nuclear families with biblical wisdom. The law of unintended consequences, of course, interrupted his well-meaning initiative. Some came to look to the family as our refuge from the storms of secularism and social confusion.

However, as blessed as the family is, a family—as we are seeing in these chapters—is not a conveyor belt of salvation. In fact, as wonderful as many families are—and with our numerous multi-generational joys from our own family—we, still, see much family dysfunction in life and mirrored in Scripture. This section of Genesis, which features Jacob fleeing from Laban, and Laban continuing his deception (plus Rachel's), is a gentle reminder not to expect too much from families. Indeed, some would occasionally welcome a little focus off the family.

Ending one family connection

The verdict from the previous verses is that Rachel stole her father's idols (v. 20), while Jacob "stole his heart"—one possible translation of "Jacob deceived him."

God, then, uses another dream in v. 24—even to speak to an apparent unbeliever. Laban, the idol worshipper and exploitative father, has a dream in which the Lord tells him not to bother or seek to correct Jacob. Following that, Laban catches up with Jacob and asks him six questions—each designed to champion poor Laban, while accusing Jacob.

Verses 26-30 contain six queries (and a threat). Laban, via those questions, accused Jacob of:

- sneaking off under the cloak of darkness,
- stealing his livestock,
- carrying off his daughters and children (as if they were his property) as plunder from battle,
- Prohibiting him from sending them off with a feast of joy and singing (right, as if he would have!),
- Preventing him from even kissing his little grandchildren,
- And then the real object (other than his coveting of livestock): why have you stolen my household gods (v. 30). That seems to be the climactic issue.

This list of doctored queries is like one of my colleagues often says: "There's the stated reason, and the *real* reason." Laban wanted his property back—including his family members—but taking his idols really got to him.

In vss. 31-34, Jacob denies that he'd taken any of Laban's tokens. Indeed, he was not guilty of this, nor privy to this. Rachel, likely out of vengeance, knew what would hurt her father the most. So she stole the household gods. Jacob welcomed a search, and while Laban searched every tent and came up empty, the final tent was Rachel's. She asked to be excused from standing due to her monthly menstruation. This far-from-ideal family has Rachel making an excuse, but she is up to her eyeballs in theft, deception, and revenge.

When no idols are found, Jacob then expresses an understandable indignation (vss 36-42). He lights into Laban, stating that Laban had changed his wages 10 times (likely there were no raises), exploited his family, and forced young Jacob to devote 20 years to starting his family. Along the way, Jacob gives credit to the providence by the God of Abraham and the "Fear of Isaac" for protecting him.

Finally, (vss 43-54), a covenant is made and witnessed by a cairn of memorial stones. In this non-aggression pact, Laban swore that he would not pursue Jacob any more by going past the heap of stones; and

Jacob swore that he would not transgress the boundary lines and raid any more livestock.

One commentator makes perceptive observations at this point about a larger issue that should concern all of us.

> Laban is a classic example of sin's irrationality (Prov. 16:2; Jer. 17:9). The deluded scoundrel, who has repeatedly cheated Jacob, unabashedly complains that Jacob has wronged him (31:26-30)! He is blind to the significance of the dream that vindicates Jacob and condemns him. He is deaf to the silence of his daughters, which shouts out against his delusion. Although he does not even attempt to rebut Jacob's evidence of innocence, he continues to claim pretentiously his right to the property and offers no apology. Contrary to all evidence, he presents himself a loving father, full of beneficence, who would send his homesick nephew and family away with song. Though he has egregiously wronged his daughters, he makes Jacob swear not to wrong them! Laban is a man without excuse . . . for hardening his heart against God out of love for himself. (Bruce Waltke, loc. cit., 436)

This tawdry episode, thus, is not only a sobering reminder about the imperfection of human families, but it is also a classic example of how sin infects families and perverts them.

Finally in v. 55, Laban makes his farewell and recedes from the literary stage. I hardly need to restate that this is far from a perfect family. It is filled with deceit, disrespect, hostility, and "grasping" (Jacob's name). All of this is the prelude toward Jacob seeking reconciliation with Esau in the next chapter.

The Out-Conniver Returns to Face his Past: Repairing Another Family Connection: (Genesis 32-33)

After a 20-year absence from Esau, Jacob now plans to go home. He has fled from Laban, but they eventually made peace of sorts. Now, he is traveling back to his home. He fully expects that Esau's anger will be unpacified. Time, after all, does not really heal all wounds.

He gathers a considerable amount of livestock—the value is massive—and sends waves of herd-offerings, along with wives and children to slake some of the pent-up anger. Jacob, of course, is projecting a wrath that he would have.

Jacob has also matured a good bit over these two decades. His prayer in 32:9-13 is a model one to illustrate true faith and praise in the OT. He addresses God as the God of his fathers; he knows God as the God of promise, and God is also the protector of him all this time. Whether it is the God of Abraham or the "Fear of Isaac," Jacob knows who this God is.

So, he attempts to ply the offended with large gifts. He sends his family over, across the Jabbok River, and spends one more night before meeting what he expects to be a still alienated brother. During this night he wrestles with a foe, who is initially thought to be a man, but later Jacob realizes this is an angel. Jacob latches on and will not release the angel until he blesses him. In the process, the angel injures Jacob's hip joint, and the author explains that is why Israelites do not eat meat attached to the hip joint. Jacob is, however, blessed, and benefits from another of those spectacular night occurrences.

He is now bolstered and ready to meet Esau. A very surprising thing happens in the narrative. As the sun rises, Jacob fords the river and thinks this may be his last day. To his amazement, Esau is thrilled to see him and runs and "falls upon his neck, and kisses him"—

language that will later be used of the parabolic father in Luke 15, who receives home his prodigal son. The phrasing indicates a full, unrestrained embrace of forgiveness. For once, Esau got something right.

While Esau was not God's choice—Jacob was (See Malachi 1), and while this does not mean that he was truly regenerate, it does show us a depiction of what real contrition is like. Esau, though condemned elsewhere, did seem to forgive his brother and they were reconciled.

Gen. 33:8-15 show Jacob's continued hesitancy, however, to believe this. It's almost too good to be true. Esau invites him back to live in the region of Seir; and Jacob agrees. However, Jacob—still wary that this might be a trap—heads a different direction to Succoth . . .

He is still, despite much maturity, deceiving. Jacob's settlement (33:16-20) leads to the next vivid and lurid chapter.

The Scandalous Rape of a Sister: A Thousand Eyes for One Eye (Genesis 34)

The Bible is a no-holds barred, raw book in sections. It does not seek to coat a veneer of glory over certain family and moral situations that are clear tokens of depravity. A scandalous rape, as well as accelerated vengeance, are presented in Genesis 34.

After Jacob settles near Shechem (perhaps he should have proceeded homeward with Esau as he said he would), the surrounding citizens desire to have Dinah, Jacob and Leah's daughter. Jacob had purchased a tract of land from Hamor (33:19). One of the sons of Hamor (likely the chieftan of the area) desired Dinah, took her against her will, and raped her. Sadly, there's nothing new under the sun.

Then Shechem, son of Hamor, decides that he wishes to marry Dinah, and Hamor asks Jacob for her hand in marriage to his son. Jacob learns about this first, while his sons were working in the pastures, and he kept this to himself at first (34:5). Hamor welcomes Jacob's family to intermarry and settle in his region.

Jacob and his sons become furious and vindictive. Rather than immediately punishing Hamor's son, Shechem, (an eye for an eye), they hatch a plan to take a thousand eyes for an eye. Indeed, what is called the *Lex Talionis* (law of fair retaliation), later enunciated as "an eye for an eye, a tooth for a tooth," may not be so much calling for vengeance as it is limiting the scope of retaliation to equity.

Notwithstanding, the lads concoct a plan, suggest it to Jacob, and Hamor agrees. These Israelites plead a religious ceremony—urging that it would not be right ("That would be a disgrace to us," v. 14b) to allow their sister to marry one who was uncircumcised. Thus, they request that circumcision be applied to all males (v. 15) in the city as a prenuptial agreement. They presented this, disingenuously of course, as a fair and mutually-beneficial plan. Hamor and Shechem went for it. They likely thought it would also be profitable (34: 23).

Hamor, like some fathers, perhaps thought that he owed his rapist-son ("the most honored" son, v. 19) a good deed, and that this high payment might straighten him out and also bring peace with the neighbors. Thus, the Shechemite males were circumcised and incapacitated for at least three days.

On the third day, the revenge—led by Simeon and Levi, Dinah's siblings—took their swords and killed every male in the city. They rescued Dinah from Shechem's house and plundered the herds and all the livestock. This ended up being a steep price for damages. All the women and children were also confiscated and enslaved.

Jacob, then, sought to rebuke his sons for expressing too much anger. Ever the pragmatist, Jacob scolds the sons who led this raid for inciting the neighbors: "You have made me a stench to the Canaanites" (v. 30). He lectures the boys that they are a minority in the area, and could be destroyed if the neighbors retaliated. While that pragmatism may not be justified, one would like to think that the scale of revenge was on Jacob's mind, but it was not mentioned.

In response, Simeon and Levi defend themselves: "Should we have treated our sister like a prostitute?" They, obviously, continued to think their slaughter was justified.

Jacob then moves on and returns to Bethel. He builds another altar (35:1). He orders them to purge their homes of any idols and to purify themselves as they approach Bethel. Bethel is remembered after all these years as a special place where God heard his prayers. After they surrendered (and buried!) their idols, as the family of Jacob marches through the region, "the terror of God" accompanied them (Bruce Waltke calls it a "panic induced holy war" as this family is now viewed as a band of "rapacious warriors."). The locals were clearly getting the message that God was on Israel's side.

"Thus, we have two cycles of duplicity going on simultaneously," writes Victor Hamilton: "Jacob's sons are deceiving Shechem and Hamor, who in turn are deceiving their own villagers. The deceivers are themselves being deceived. This scenario of double deception we may recall from earlier days in Jacob's life, where the perpetrator of deceit was also the victim of deceit." (Hamilton, 366).

On the renewal of the covenant, this is very similar to Genesis 17. In each:

- God appears (17:1; 35:9) and later disappears (17:22; 35:13).
- The same divine name (El Shaddai) is employed (17:1; 35:11).
- A name change occurs—Abram → Abraham in 17:5); Jacob → Israel (35:10).
- The promises of successors, rulers, and land grants are given (17:6-8; 35: 11-12).

God is the same with his people, even weak or deceitful people, and his covenant is the same.

Isaac's death is clarified (harmonized with Hamilton, 389):

- Isaac is 60 at the birth of the twins (25:26).
- Isaac was 100 when Esau married (26:34).
- Isaac thought he might be on the verge of death (ch. 27), with fading eyesight, but he clearly lived much longer.
- Isaac would have been ca 120 when Esau and Jacob were reconciled (31:41)
- Isaac was 180 years old at his death.

Isaac would have lived almost six decades after his sons were reconciled. The Scripture provides very little information on this period of history, moving us toward the Joseph cycle in chapters 37-50.

On Genealogies: A Test of 2 Tim. 3:16, I Cor 10:11 (Genesis 35-36)

Beginning a book or Testament with a genealogy sounds like a snoozer. Yet, many family-accounts are included in the Bible. Pause for a short minute with me to consider a few things about these.

Most people think these are boring; unless it affects me.
Mormons put a lot of stock in these, but most people don't. Recently, I had a relative become very interested in his lineage, primarily because he had been adopted.

Still, while some may enjoy this hobby, most people are too busy, too present-oriented, or too self-absorbed to care that much about the past. And I do not suggest that knowing all about genealogies is fun.

Most of us read through the Bible like a computer spell check program. Many of us read the Bible that way—blazing through as quickly as we can, as if a prize were given to the one who finishes first. This "auto pilot" style of Bible reading, in which we zap out the commercials, skips over the hard or the non-sensational.

We chug on along at high speed, crunching the biblical truths, skipping over great portions of gospel until we come to a section that slows us down. In that process we breeze over many timeless nuggets. Some of the most skipped portions in Bibles are the genealogies. Few people ever slow down in those sections. Instead, when we get to one of those 'begat' sections, we crank up the reading speed, and in overdrive we accelerate right on past the boiled-down history of entire generations.

According to some, "Me" always comes first. If I don't get a spiritual "buzz" or chills down my spine, then obviously this part of the Bible is not very important. It must 'turn me on' or 'push my buttons.' To hear some talk, it's almost as if the amount of Scripture which folks endorse is dependent on whether or not, it makes one feel good. Is that the standard we want to cultivate . . . that this is God's Word if and only if it lights me up; and if not, don't bother?

Imagine, that there are parts of the Bible, or parts of the Christian life that may not be scintillating, pure-fun, and as thrilling as attending a major playoff game! Where did we ever get this notion that everything in life must be entertaining, interesting, or sensational, or else be rejected as boring? Other Christians in other parts of the world, say China, or a former Eastern European nation do not hold such prerequisites.

Notwithstanding, the fact that all genealogies are not thrilling does not mean they are unimportant.

1. There are two early genealogies in this book—chapters 5 and 11.

The first of those traces how death came to all. It reinforces God's promise that "in the day you eat of the fruit, you will die." Genesis 5 shows how inescapable that is, tracing the first family from Adam to Noah.

God wishes to provide connective material.

Then, chapter 11 contains the genealogy that traces from Noah to Abram. The Lord seems to want to tell his people that they come from some family. We don't just arise out of nothing.

2. There are even genealogies of the non-patriarchs.

Ishmael (25) and Esau (36) are even included. And these were not the good boys of the OT. What does that tell us? Well, at least, that God cares about people, even if they are not from a chosen family.

It is surprising to see Ishmael's line included, but he is still an offspring of Abraham. Even more surprising is the listing of Esau in Genesis 36. Few of his descendants are famous. This chapter covers the following:

36:1-19   The Family of Esau and the Chiefs of Edom
36:20-30   The Family of Seir (a near neighbor)
36:31-39   The Kings of Edom; these were early judges, not dynastic monarchs.
36:40-43   The chiefs of Esau.

What do we learn from the inclusion of this non-favored line?

a. God cares for many, even imperfect families.
  b. History is important, even for the unbelieving line.
  c. Continuity, heritage explains some things.

3. *Genealogies of Grace in the Gospel (cf. Mt. 1:1-7)*
   From this NT genealogy, we may learn the following.

A. Each biblical genealogy contains a central theological message.

For example, the genealogy in Genesis 5 underscores the message that, arising from sin, inevitably death occurs. The depressing refrain, at the end of each generation is...

___lived ___number of years, AND HE DIED. (Repeat). That genealogy and every one had a central theological thrust. There is a message to these 'begats.'

So what is the message of this one in Matthew, leading to the birth of our Savior? The message of this genealogy is that *God uses people based on his grace, not on their merit.* Our God consistently uses the mode of grace to work his plan out in this world. He has never used human ability, moral perfection, nor family inheritance alone to be the chief factor in leading to Jesus' birth or anything else.

B. Women, who are especially singled out as exemplars of Grace.

1. The five females listed in this genealogy are: Tamar (v. 3), Rahab (v. 5), Ruth (v. 5), Uriah's wife- Bathsheba (v. 6), and Mary (v. 16).

2. All of these had at least one thing in common . . . bad reputation. None of these escaped life unscathed. Each of these in her own way, even though several were pure as the driven rain, were harshly criticized.

3. Further, most were accused of a notorious sin, e. g., sexual immorality.

The always-helpful J. C. Ryle concludes with three lessons in his commentary on this passage.

> We learn, for one thing, from this list of names, that God always keeps His word. He had promised that "in Abraham's seed all the nations of the earth should be blessed." He had promised to raise up a Savior of the family of David. (Gen. 12:3; Is. 11:1.) These sixteen verses prove that Jesus was the son of David and the Son of Abraham, and that

God's promise was fulfilled. Thoughtless and ungodly people should remember this lesson, and be afraid. Whatever they may think, God will keep His word. If they repent not, they will surely perish. True Christians should remember this lesson, and take comfort. Their Father in heaven will be true to all His engagements. He has said that He will save all believers in Christ. If He has said it, He will certainly do it. "He is not a man, that He should lie." "He abideth faithful: He cannot deny Himself." (Num. 23:19; 2 Tim. 2:13.)

We learn, for another thing, from this list of names, the sinfulness and corruption of human nature. It is instructive to observe how many godly parents in this catalogue had wicked and ungodly sons. The names of Rehoboam, and Joram, and Amon, and Jechonias, should teach us humbling lessons. They had all pious fathers. But they were all wicked men. Grace does not run in families. It needs something more than good examples and good advice to make us children of God. They that are born again are not born of blood, nor of the will of the flesh, nor of the will of man, but of God. (John i.13.) Praying parents should pray night and day, that their children may be born of the Spirit.

We learn, lastly, from this list of names, how great is the mercy and compassion of our Lord Jesus Christ. Let us think how defiled and unclean human nature is, and then think what a condescension it was in Him to be born of a woman, and made in the "like-ness of men." (Phil. 2:7) Some of the names we read in this catalogue remind us of shameful and sad histories. Some of the names are those of persons never mentioned elsewhere in the Bible. But at the end of all comes the names of the Lord Jesus Christ. Though He is the eternal God, He humbles Himself to become man, in order to provide salvation for sinners. "Though He was rich, yet for your sakes He became poor." (2 Cor. 8:9.)

We should always read this catalogue with thankful feelings. We see here that no one who partakes of human nature can be beyond the reach of Christ's sympathy and compassion. Our sins may have been as black and great as those of any whom St. Matthew names. But they cannot shut us out of heaven, if we repent and believe the Gospel. If the Lord Jesus was not ashamed to be born of a woman whose pedigree contained such names as those we have read today, we need not think that He will be ashamed to call us brethren, and to give us eternal life.

A Brat and his Brothers' Deception (Genesis 37)

This is an episode about a teenager who goes from family privilege to pit to palace to prison to prominence. Finally, he goes to provider to prevent the line of the Messiah from being extinguished by a famine. It is also a diary of family dysfunction and parenting mistakes. Through it all, however, God's hand is at work and underneath are the everlasting arms.

One commentator summarized: *The Jacob cycle is about rocks; the Joseph cycle is about robes.*

Bruce Waltke's outline (494) of this final 'book within a book' (*toledoth*) stresses "conflict."

       Gen. 37-38 The family in conflict in Canaan
       Gen. 39-41 Joseph in conflict with imperial power in Egypt
       Gen. 42-44 The family in conflict in Canaan and Egypt
       Gen. 45-47 The family conflict resolved in Egypt
       Gen. 48-50 The conflict over, the family blessed in Egypt, looking to Canaan.

The theme that we have been describing is repeated again here: God's sovereign plan is not disturbed even by weak characters, sinful strife within a family, nor evil plottings. The final quarter of the book of Genesis begins in chapter 37, focusing on Jacob's descendants, chiefly Joseph. It concludes with this enduring lesson: When evil men or forces intend ill, God still works that for good, as the NT text in Romans 8:28 tells us.

This passage is a classic text on the providence of God. It is a long narrative showing how God's providence is woven through and through. Derek Kidner writes: "It also exhibits, as, Stephen was to show, a human pattern that runs through the OT to culminate at

Calvary: the rejection of God's chosen deliverers, through the envy and unbelief of their kith and kin—yet a rejection which is finally made to play its own part in bringing about deliverance." (179)

Joseph is introduced in the opening 4 verses of this chapter. After Jacob settled his family, Joseph clearly became his favorite—so much so that Jacob showed it by weaving an ornate robe for Joseph. This was likely a symbol similar to that used by kings for dynastic succession. Joseph was dubbed the "prince" at the age of 17.

And he did not always model the maturity that he showed later. We do need to permit teenagers to have some imperfections but by God's sanctifying grace to outgrow such.

Joseph's siblings reacted as expected: they resented Joseph, they despised him, and they probably were pretty miffed at their father for such overt favoritism. Surely, it goes without much more comment to note that parents should appreciate all the differences of their children but not dub favorites.

Joseph, then, at the age of 17 has a dream. His father was known for these a generation earlier, and this may be another part of the succession plan: Jacob wanted the "dreamer" son to carry on his legacy. Joseph has two dreams recorded in these verses.

First, in v. 7, he has a dream with agrarian symbolism. Various sheafs of grain are gathered, and one rises up with the others bowing down to it. Joseph is understood as telling his brothers that he will rule over them, and they will bow down to him. Their hatred only grew.

His second dream added a layer of subservience from his family. In this dream, set in the celestial world, eleven stars bow down to him, along with the son and the moon also. The clear meaning, which leads to even more enmity and jealousy, is that not only will the eleven brothers bow down to Joseph, but so will mom and dad.

Jacob is none too pleased with this and rebukes Joseph. Of course, by the final chapter of Genesis these dream's predictions come true. However, the way Joseph presented these was likely an indication of his immaturity and it only made things worse. Jacob filed this away, but the brothers would look for ways to put the baby brother in his place.

Understandable resentment is seen in the family (cf vss. 4-5, 10-11). Joseph begins with a position of privilege, but in the remainder of the chapter, we will see his first "down cycle" as he ends up in a pit and is trafficked by his own brothers (37:12- 36).

Father Jacob likely realizes that Joseph had been sheltered and should assume more duties in the family livestock business. So, he commissions Joseph on an errand to visit his brothers and to see how things are going—then to report back. Joseph blithely goes off on this errand.

At first, he cannot locate the shepherds or flock and is sent to Dothan—several days away from home. With very little self-awareness, as he approaches his brothers, he is dressed in the garb that incenses them so much. From a distance they quickly spy his ornamental outerwear and mock, "here comes that dreamer." It is possible that for many nights under the stars, they had discussed plans for revenge, for they quickly come up with a plan.

The brothers, first, say "let's kill him," fake the death, and take a bloody robe to dad. However, one brother seeks to show a little mercy. Reuben suggests that they merely throw him into a cistern and move on, allowing him to die but telling themselves that they are not actively murderers. This notion buys a temporary halt. Joseph, remember, likely heard all these conversations.

Jealousy, hatred, and revenge drive these brothers, and Reuben moves off stage to attend to some errand or duty. He sought to show some mercy.

The next brother, Judah, appears mercenary. He sees a caravan from Midian and adds to the plot a financial motive. He suggests that they not murder their brother-Dreamer (not because he has compassion on Joseph) but that, avoiding such technically, they also make some money in the process. Judah proposes that they sell Joseph for the normal price of a man's life: 20 shekels of silver. He is clearly being trafficked, and the purchase price is agreed to.

Joseph is sold to a caravan of Ishmaelites for this price, and then the brothers hatch a final level of deception: to cover the robe with goat blood and return it to father Jacob as proof that they had not murdered the baby brother.

Worth noting, rather than a contradiction (supposedly by clumsy editors), the Midianites and Ishmaelites were names that often were interchangeable. That the Midianites could equally be described as

Ishmaelites may be seen from Judges 8:22-28. These names are used interchangeably with Ishmaelite being "the more generic term, while "Midianite" is the more specific and ethnic term." (Hamilton, 423)

The plot is nearly complete. Reuben returns and is very distraught that the brother is not in the pit. The brothers explain their trafficking plot to him, and then they conspire to fake a death. They kill an animal, cover Joseph's ornamental robe with blood, and take it home to dad, asking him to verify that this is Joseph's robe. One must note the concluding irony of Jacob being deceived by an exterior covering with animal blood on it, as he tricked his father years ago.

Parents might all wish to learn from this, in the words of former President Reagan, to "trust but verify" the stories of your children.

Jacob is so distressed that he is willing to go down to the grave to his favored son. He does not wish to go on with life, and the chapter concludes by telling us that Joseph is eventually bought by Potiphar. Joseph has gone from privilege to the pit in this chapter. In chapter 39, as the narrative resumes, he will rise to a prominent palace.

But first, chapter 38 will provide an interlude showing more family scandal, depravity, and deceit.

Acts 7:9-10 confirms the historicity, indicating that this is far from mythical or a propagandistic narrative. These scandals and deceptions were as real as any other history in Genesis.

A Strong Female Gets Justice (Genesis 38)
How Do I Defraud Thee, Let me Count the Ways

To follow this narrative, I wish to recount the various acts of fraud or deceit in this single chapter. It shows us a woman who was truly misused . . . and how she obtains justice. This will be a strong contrast to the next chapter. Yet, it shows us also how God protects the righteous (38:26).

Judah, one of the 12 sons of Jacob, was the one who concocted the scheme in the previous chapter to sell Joseph for profit, instead of murdering him. Judah is now isolated in this chapter, which breaks the flow of the narrative—chapter 39 picks up right where chapter 37 left off.

Why the narrative interruption? One commentator answers that this episode would not fit stylistically at the end of the Joseph cycle and must be put here. Another speculates that the location of this narrative here supports the fact that wandering off from one's covenant family and settling near unbelievers (see Lot above) can lead to problems. It is also definitely about the Messianic line.

Derek Kidner sets this "rude interruption of the Joseph story" in context as follows: "It creates suspense for the reader, with Joseph's future in the balance; it puts the faith and chastity of Joseph, soon to be described, in a context which sets off their rarity; and it fills out the portrait of the effective leader among the ten brothers." (187)

Judah's wife and sons introduced (1-5)

Judah settles close to a friend from Hirah (Adullam) in Canaanite territory and takes a Canaanite wife, described only as the daughter of Shua. Judah and his wife have three sons: Er, Onan, and Shelah. In time, Judah seeks a wife for each of these three. He sets his eye of Tamar, and she becomes the wife of Er.

Er was wicked in the Lord's sight—we don't know what particular wickedness—and the Lord takes his life. That leaves Tamar as a widow. According to later Hebrew legislation (cf. also Mt. 22:23-33) in Dt. 25:5ff, if a brother dies leaving no male child, his brother is to step up and marry the widow, protectively taking her into his home and furnishing a son through the widow. Such son would legally be and carry on the name of the deceased brother. This was established as a duty and to perpetuate the line, not to encourage bigamy.

Judah's sons were under this duty, but the second son (Onan) intentionally avoided this duty. Judah instructed Onan to take Tamar to be his wife and produce offspring with her, but Onan (who understood procreation well in 1800 BC) did not fulfill his duty to Tamar. Instead of consummating the marriage and producing offspring, he contraceptively prevented conception (v. 9). The Lord, however, was not fooled and took Judah's second son's life (Gen. 38:10).

Observing the loss of his first two sons associated with Tamar, Judah decided not to risk his third son (Shelah) and sought to care for her in his own home (as a widow) until Shelah grew up. The time lapse could easily have been 15 years. Suffice it to say that Tamar did not believe she was being treated righteously.

Judah Tricked

Judah's solution for widowhood and Tamar's quick deceit are depicted in Gen. 38:12-19) "The trick Tamar played against Judah is a response to the trick Judah played against Tamar." (Hamilton, 441). After Judah's wife dies, he goes up to Timnah with his fraternity buddy, Adullam, at the time of sheep shearing. These times were known as rowdy times, with carousing fairly accepted.

Tamar finds out about it (we're not told how she learned this) and positions herself along the route where Judah is expected. She knew that year after year had passed, and Judah-Shelah were not keeping their duty to pass on the family line. So, running ahead of Judah, she swaps her widow's garments and presents herself like a prostitute, along with a veil to conceal her true identity. Judah, like a sheep heading to slaughter, is a fairly easy target. He solicits her, agrees to pay her a young goat, but of course does not have that goat with him. Tamar, who has planned this out, asks for some pledge. Cooperative, panting Judah agrees to her request: to give her his seal, cord, and staff (v. 18)—three items that were clearly his unique property.

She secures these, has sex with Judah (although oddly is never recognized), and becomes pregnant. She then disappears, returns home, and resumes her widow role (v.19).

Judah then send Adullam, his emissary, with goat in hand to pay the prostitute. After Adullam inquires and does due diligence, none of the locals know of such a shrine prostitute. Thus, Adullam explains this to Judah, who does not wish to risk more embarrassment, and maintains that he has sought to pay the prostitute. He cannot help it that she cannot be located. So, Judah returns home and goes about his business, thinking that he's all squared.

However, three months later, it is learned that Tamar is pregnant. Judah in a fit of hypocrisy calls for her not merely to receive the death penalty (stoning was the norm for adultery) but to be incinerated—so evil was she. Judah exclaims: "Bring here out and have her burned to death."

As she comes before him, she brings his seal, cord, and staff—which she'd carefully kept—and asks him if he recognizes there. He is immediately convicted and pronounces "she is more righteous than I." (v. 26) And not only does he confess his sin, but he makes it right (finally!) but giving Tamar to his son Shelah. Duty is finally fulfilled.

Shortly thereafter, she gives birth to twins. In another case of twins vying for the first birth, Zerah crowns slightly earlier, with the midwife tying a scarlet thread around his hand, but Perez (the other twin) is delivered first. Perez will later appear at the end of the Book of Ruth in the genealogy leading to Jesus.

Tamar, remember, is a Canaanite woman (Mt. 1:3), who rescues the line of Judah. Tamar in Jesus' genealogy illustrates how God works, even amidst "whispers of scandal." This is a similar plotline to the Book of Ruth. God uses a non-Hebrew woman, associated with immorality, to preserve the line of Messiah. If not for her strong action (and manipulation!), the line of Jesus might have died out. The next chapter resumes that story as God raises up Joseph to keep the line of Messiah going, this time through a devastating famine.

But to conclude this episode, note a few similarities and contrasts. Judah is accustomed to using women and not fulfilling his duty to care for them. He thinks he's done nothing wrong. King David was similar. In both cases, Cf. 2 Sam 12, a powerful man is confronted with his sin. Judah and David both react initially with self-righteous indignation. "Burn the whore," says Judah. But then he is convicted of his sin and has to admit that she was more righteous than he was. David also had to admit that to Nathan over the Bathsheba travesty.

There are also several contrasts between these chapters (38 and 39), which may speak a bit to why the narrative is placed where it is.

- Tamar (38) is a seductress, but is said to be righteous. Mrs. Potiphar (39) was only predatory.
- Judah (38) seeks sexual involvement. Joseph (39) flees from it.
- Jacob weeps over his lost son, Joseph (37:34). Judah tries to cover up and move on.

Scripture often portrays how quick we are to vindicate ourselves. It's easy to spot the sins of others, especially when pregnancy makes such undeniable. But our sins find us out, too.

#NotTrue (Genesis 39)

Joseph was sold by his brothers to wandering caravans. He ended up being a slave to a ranking Egyptian official, Potiphar. It looks as if he's been rescued and will rise to heights again. However, on the way up, he is harassed by Mrs. Potiphar, falsely accused, and ends up in jail. He was accused of rape; only it was #NotTrue.

Frequently, women are in a vulnerable state with powerful men forcing them into sexual acts against their will. In this chapter, we see the reverse: a powerful woman, seeking to force a younger man into a sexual act. And when that does not succeed, the powerful woman accuses young Joseph of rape.

This chapter includes a narrative of hope, amidst questions about despair. Those questions help us drill down into a few practical issues.

There is an outline that shows the alternating rise and fall of Joseph:

1A Exalted in Potiphar's house (39:1-6)
 1B Brought down to prison (39:7-20)
 2A Exalted in the Prison warden's house (39:21-23)
 2B Brought down again (and forgotten) as an imprisoned slave (40:1-23)

In the opening verse, Joseph is sold into the home of a leading official: Pharaoh's captain of the guard. Potiphar was the chief law enforcement official of the palace. He oversaw the prisons and had risen to a position of high trust and respect. He was also likely wealthy. He purchased Joseph—a strapping late teenager—and put him to work in his estate.

Along the way, Joseph rose in prominence from slave to trusted overseer. All that he did seemed to be blessed by the Lord. There is no evidence, of course, that prior to this Potiphar was either a believer in anything other than the Egyptian religion of the day. Yet, Potiphar himself ascribed to Jahweh the blessings that Joseph brought. Joseph's success led to even more trust. Before he is accused, he is put in charge of everything in Potiphar's household, except the food preparation. V. 7 notes that Joseph was handsome and had a fine physique. One may wonder, even, if Mrs. Potiphar might have accompanied her husband to the slave market and handpicked the ripped young Hebrew.

Verses 7-9 the describe Mrs. Potiphar's propositions and Joseph's denials. When she overtly invited him to sleep with her, Joseph exhibits a strong resolve that is very uncharacteristic for teenage males at that age. He provides two reasons that he will not have sex with her: (1) first, it would dishonor his master, who had promoted him and entrusted so much to him—Joseph will not betray Potiphar for this; and (2) secondly, it is morally "wicked" and a "sin" against God. Joseph new that adultery was a sin, called it such, and resisted it—even with an influential and likely beautiful woman.

What would this young man have to do to offset this temptation? He knew what was wrong; he thought ahead, and did not cave in. Young people (all people, really) need to plan ahead and be prepared to say "no" to sexual immorality—even when it is freely available.

However, Mrs. Potiphar is persistent. She had planned this and propositions Joseph again and again. Can a female be the initiator of such immorality? If you don't think so, simply return to Proverbs 7:12-21 (and other Proverbs), where the adulteress is clearly depicted. She is a loud gadabout, going around, approaching an unsuspecting male, telling him that her husband is away, and that he is amazing, and that she has even purchased pre-forgiveness by paying her vows. Plus, she has the perfume and the fine linen sheets. This woman is on the prowl and many males would succumb to her.

Joseph, however, does not! He resists the temptation and flees from her, leaving his cloak in her hand. With that, she quickly plots revenge and accuses Joseph of attempted rape. She tells the servants (and any who would listen) that this Hebrew was mocking her and attempted to have forced sex with her. She claims to have screamed (which she did not) and has kept the cloak as proof of his immorality.

She spreads her false accusation widely, and makes her false accusation to her husband (vss 16-18). She has a convincing story, supposed proof (the cloak), and motive: 'he is making sport of us.' Potiphar is understandably angry; and throws Joseph in prison. As Joseph goes from palace to prison—and Potiphar, remember, knew the prison system and leaders well—a question occurs: Why did Potiphar not seek the death penalty? It easily could have been carried out.

Perhaps, Potiphar saw potential in Joseph and had mercy on him. It is also possible that Potiphar questioned some of his wife's fidelity.

While in prison, God exalts Joseph again in vss 21-2. Joseph is blessed and succeeds even in prison.

The mistress of the house is "a slave to her lust for her husband's slave." (Hamilton, 560) Also, a slave was viewed as the property of the owner and could not refuse orders. Joseph, though terribly vulnerable, resisted this temptation.

Do males always tell the truth about their sexual escapades? Of course not. Are females somehow removed from the tendencies of sin in the area of false accusations? Or put the question this way: Is either gender more inherently truthful or moral than the other? A review of female dishonesty just in this first book alone reminds us that:

- Eve distorted the truth and was not inherently more honest than Adam.
- Sarah participated in the deception, passing herself off as Abraham's sister—twice!—and so did Rebekah later.
- Lot's daughters, while their comments were not used to deceive their father, initiated and participated in immoral activity, without being pressured to do so, except from their own rationalization. Their mother also had far too much attraction to Sodom.
- Sarah initially doubted that God could produce a child in her womb. When he confronted her, she dissembled and tried to deny it.
- Rebekah blatantly deceived Isaac in order to get the blessing for Jacob.
- Laban's daughters participated in many deceptions. Rachel even lied and stole her father's cherished idols.
- Tamar set Judah up for a fall, represented herself as a prostitute, and with premeditation used her words to mislead Judah, even though she was righteous.

These things being true just from the first book of the Bible, we could find many other examples.

The point is this: women should be protected, honored, and cherished. They are not, however, sinless nor from another verbal universe. Women and men both:

- Can deceive
- Can use their words to cloak their real agenda
- Can falsely accuse another
- Can extol their own virtues
- Can frame a vulnerable person out of revenge.

Sin does not exempt either gender.

We see from this episode "God's quiet control and the man of faith's quiet victory." (Kidner, 189)

In sum, Joseph thought he was as low as he could go after being rejected by his brothers and sold as a slave. However, the Lord blessed him and exalted him in Potiphar's household. Then, he was imprisoned (wrongly so) for rape and sunk even lower than originally. At first, he was a slave, without any civic protections. In prison, he was a slave and a criminal, without any civic protections. Would he blame or reject God?

This pattern of exaltation and humiliation is also a type, a taste, of the experience of Jesus, the Messianic descendent of Jacob's line.

From Prison Back to the Palace: The Dreamer is Exalted (Genesis 40-41)

Joseph serves God, even in dire circumstances.

Joseph has landed in prison because of a false accusation. While in prison, he meets two other chief officials from Pharaoh's court: the cupbearer and the chief baker. Both of these would be intimates of Pharaoh—the baker prepared the food, and the cupbearer was a trusted last defense from assassination by poisoning. These men would see Pharaoh daily, but he was displeased with them and put them in jail.

Not by accident, they were lodged in the same jail as Joseph. Joseph was highly trusted by the chief warden. In the progress of time, both the cupbearer and baker had dreams. They could not interpret the meaning of these dreams and were disturbed and agitated over these dreams.

Joseph had earlier displayed his spiritual gift of interpreting dreams—to the chagrin of his family members (cf. Gen. 37 above). Now in jail, when he inquired about the reasons for anxiety from the dreams of the cupbearer and baker, Joseph was able to interpret their dreams.

The cupbearer's dream involved grapes being turned into wine, and Joseph interpreted that as Pharaoh restoring the cupbearer to his trusted position within three days. The baker's dream involved grain (which would be turned to bread) and birds eating the grain as he carried it in a basket on his head. Joseph interpreted this dream that Pharaoh would restore the baker to his position within three days but would hang him—off with his head.

Both dreams had similarities, but Joseph did not give the same outcome for each dream. He was certainly not a 'prosperity gospel' prophet who interpreted all things as uniformly positive.

After three days, both officials were restored to Pharaoh's court. The cupbearer continued in service, but (as predicted) the baker was hung or impaled on a tree after his head was lopped off. Moreover, the only request that Joseph made for his dream interpretation was ignored by Pharaoh's officials. Joseph was forgotten (for over two years), while they were set free. However, he will not remain in jail. As with an earlier scene, again "Joseph is brought up from a dungeon; again, his ability to interpret dreams plays a crucial role in his fate; again, he finds himself in charge of a house, this time Pharaoh's!" (Waltke, 529)

Joseph's view of and witness to God

Throughout this winding narrative, Joseph takes every opportunity to talk about God and reflect his view of God. Among the things that we may glean from this section are:

a. Only God gives interpretation (40:9b; 41:16; 41:25) of dreams. Joseph is not seeking to bring attention to himself or a ministry.
b. God decrees (41:25, 28, "firmly decided" in v. 32), and his sovereign decrees are fixed. Joseph knows God as all-powerful and not beholden to any.
c. The Spirit of God was living in Joseph (41:38). Joseph's life and ministry are driven by the Holy Spirit, who acted for centuries before Christ. The real explanation for Joseph's success is the working of the Spirit in him.
d. God makes even unbelievers listen. Joseph's service and character shine through the shadows of falsehood and fakery so much that even those who are not Hebrews had to take notice.

God is using this young man, even in the worst of situations to provide for his family and the line that would lead to Messiah. Along the way, Joseph gives clear tribute to God, and his neighbors see this.

Joseph's wisdom: from God

Pharaoh, too, had some upsetting dreams. He has two successive dreams—one involving cattle, the other involving grain. In each dream, a cycle of sevens is given. In the first dream, Pharaoh saw 7 fat cows, which were eventually devoured by 7 lean, gaunt cows. In the second dream, Pharaoh saw 7 bundles of grain that were abundant, eventually overtaken by 7 rotten bundles of grain. He, like the baker and cupbearer earlier, could not interpret the dreams. And he was perplexed and disturbed. He called in all his court prophets, and none could interpret.

Presto, whamo, after two years, the cupbearer remembered Joseph and his ability to interpret dreams. He told Pharaoh this, and Pharaoh sent for Joseph, who cleaned up before meeting with the king.

Joseph gave credit to God for the gift of interpretation and inquired about the dreams. Pharaoh relayed those to him, and Joseph had a fairly quick interpretation, in stark contrast to the fake prophets. He told Pharaoh that these dreams—in duplicate to show the fixedness of this—meant that the next 7 years would be a time of abundance, both for livestock and grain, but that the 7 years after that would be a time of famine and scarcity. Accordingly, a disciplined savings plan was needed empire-wide.

Pharaoh appreciated the dream's interpretation, quickly agreed to it, and sought to plan accordingly. Joseph not only interpreted the dream but also gave advice on how to survive from the coming famine.

The features of this plan were as follows:
- 20% of Harvest or 140% (from 41:37 might it not have been 160% or so?) was to be collected and stored in advance.
- Grain was to be saved and stored in designated cities.
- After the 7 banner years of abundance, the stored grain was to be used gradually during 7 lean years, selling it to the people with profit to Pharaoh (41:56)
- Surplus allowed sales to non-Egyptians (41:57).

This plan would eventually benefit Jacob's family, and the line leading to Messiah would not be starved out due to the famine.

Joseph is a striking example of what the Apostle Paul describe in Philippians 4:12-14. Writing from prison (where he also had been falsely accused), Paul spoke for all Christians as he said that he knew what it was like to be content in plenty or in want. Whether full and well-fed, or whether framed and frustrated with limitations, Paul kept his eye on the Sovereign God and, rather than complain or grumble, he patiently waited for the Lord to work.

Like Joseph earlier, the apostle to the Gentiles had also been released from prison (See Acts 16:22 ff), and he knew that it was better to fix his trust on God than on any ruler, princes, or jailers. Any who are persecuted for righteousness sake should be comforted by knowing that God knows and cares for his children.

Economics and Politics During a Famine: Sovereignty in Action[23]

Hundreds of years after Joseph's bitter experience, Psalm 105 confirms the historicity of the account we find in Genesis. It refers clearly to all these events in the latter chapters of Genesis.

Joseph was elevated to Prime Minister—rising from "Potiphar's house to the jailhouse to Pharaoh's house." (Hamilton, 508) A review of his chronology might help put things in some perspective. The verses below inform us about his age at various stages in this narrative.

37:2 Age 17
40:14, 23 Age 28 (interpreted dreams and then forgotten, to remain in prison)
41:1, 46 Age 30
45:6 Age 39

Joseph was sold into slavery about 1800 BC. After a series of personal ascents and descents, he served several government administrations at various levels. By the end of his life, he was a high official in the court of Pharaoh. Genesis 41 and 47 are also instructive on matters of state. Joseph, by divine charisma, was able to interpret Pharaoh's troubling dream about seven fat cows and seven lean cows. The interpretation was that for the next 14 years Egypt would have cycles of plenty and want. For the first seven years, the cattle and crops would be abundant. The second seven years, however, would be characterized by severe famine. If some form of pre-savings plan was not implemented the people would starve; in fact, many did.

---

[23] Note; some of this section is taken from *Savior or Servant*, chapter 2, used with permission.

Joseph advised Pharaoh to use "commissioners" (Gen. 41:34) to store up essential natural resources ahead of time. These commissioners were to take 20% of the crops during the abundant period. This taxation would still leave the people with sufficient food, when the abundance was taken into account. Joseph stored away the grain in centralized cities (Gen. 41:35), held it in reserve, and was put in charge of this program.

The presumption is that this plan was acceptable to the Lord. Nowhere is it condemned by God; only commended by the citizens. Still, insofar as this example touches on the areas of taxation and state protocol, this narrative set of precedents must be harmonized with other didactic principles. Yet, it does give an example of a benevolent administration with the prudence to prepare for times of scarcity. The tax rate for this national emergency, although twice the rate of the tithe, was only temporary and did not prevent normal commerce. One could even see this taxation as a collection of the surplus especially provided by God. In light of the abundance, the people retained virtually the normal amount of goods, contributing mainly from the divinely-produced excess.

This narrative acknowledges a place for wise, cooperative government. From this model, the following principles can be established (and developed in more detail below):

1. *Responsibility (both personal and as encouraged by the government) for saving for the future is delegated.*
2. *There is a role in catastrophic times for a centralized government.*
3. *It is also worthy of note that in this episode there is an international result* (Gen. 41:57).
4. *Also present in this model is a collective* (Gen. 47:13-27).

Even though many modern states have encroached on other divinely-ordained agencies—sometimes nearly smothering them—one must be careful not to over-react and disregard the divinely approved precedents provided in Scripture. The dangers of leviathan-states are writ large in our century; however, there are benefits of centralizing methods which occasionally help, as long as they do not violate any other divine prerogative or become useful only for the administrators or their sub-delegates. Centralization as a method of economical stewardship is not wrong; only when centralization crushes the vitality of other spheres is it dangerous.

From this model, the following principles can be established.

1. *Responsibility (both personal and as encouraged by the government) for saving for the future is delegated.* In consumerist societies, it has often been pointed out that the lack of future planning, as well as a low personal saving rate, is detrimental to the economic health of a culture. In this case, it is instructive to see that the first step in providing for basic necessities was to encourage limited consumption during the good years in order to save for the lean years. This is a principle that would assist any state. Both personal and governmental responsibility are shared toward this end. On an irreducible level, even if the government does not encourage this prudence, the family should implement this on a small scale. Personal and familial responsibility in this area is fundamental.

It might even be acceptable for the state to require personal savings plans (as some countries do) with such plans administered by the private sector, with the responsibility remaining in the hands of the individual. Most who object to a nationalized "Social Security" do not object in principle to forced savings *per se*; they object to the state assuming financial support for others *via* a collectivist method, or the unwise investments or unsound actuarial bases of such systems. This episode in the life of Joseph may not be stretched to require support for such "Social Security" measures. However, it does support the state playing a role in providing for the future safety of its citizens. It is also crucial to keep the taxation rates limited, to not expropriate the needed provisions for families and individuals, and to have the support of the people.

2. *There is a role in catastrophic times for a centralized government.* Some may argue that this is an exception, rather than the rule in light of its catastrophic nature. That is possible. A maxim of historical study is that norms should be carefully established when taken from exceptional eras of history. Nevertheless, it is clear from Genesis 41:34 that Joseph proposed a centralized system for this emergency. The origination of this centralization is neither attributable

to secular origin nor due to statist imposition. On the contrary, the suggestion emanates from divine revelation and the godly counsel from Joseph himself. If the central government was *never* to be involved—even in emergency situations like these—then surely God would not have sanctioned this instance. Yet with divine blessing, there is a proper role for administrative centralization. This particular administrative plan even went to preserve the line of the Messiah. Administrative centralization should not be considered an *a priori* evil; it depends on the agents involved and the extent of governmental sweep.

Care should be taken, however, in application, since this may be such an exceptional era. It is not dangerous to admit some necessary centralization of administration. In fact, good stewardship of finite resources demands such. It is only dangerous to surrender responsibility exclusively or permanently to the wrong agency. In this (temporary) episode, at least it is possible to allow some state activity while not permanently relegating the care for citizens to the state. While this passage does not mandate or justify statist control of food or commerce, unless one imposes an interpretation on the Scriptures, possible helpful synergy can be admitted. Theologically, it is not the case that the state *per se* is inherently evil or to be avoided. It is only the improper usurpation by the state, or the lawless activity of the state that is prohibited. Christians wish to avoid devaluing the state, just as they hate to see the church devalued. Both are proper institutions of God and should be encouraged to perform their lawful role as defined by other Scriptures. Government has its proper place.

The above notwithstanding, a sincere caveat must be issued for this interpretation. It must be mitigated by the criticism of seeking to derive an "ought" from an "is." The above interpretation is open to the charge of seeking to draw inferences from the historical set of events. These structures may be exceptional, non-normal, and unable to be used for extrapolation. In an attempt to be fair to the record, this should at least be mentioned as a possibility, although dogmatism at this point would surely be incautious.

If the state adhered to other divine principles (which is often not the case), activity as described in this narrative would not be threatening.

3. *It is also worthy of note that in this episode there is an international result* (Gen. 41:57). This episode makes it clear that not only does a good policy aid its own citizens, but moreover it is respected and valued by other nations. Perhaps one of the criteria for measurable success in policy reform is the extent to which other nations wish to model their political systems after the ones that do work. This can best be seen in times of international crisis. If it is a poor model, it may work only with limited cultural adaptation. If it is a successful model, it will likely have universal applicability. Cicero once wrote that the best governments would not "lay down one rule at Rome and another at Athens, nor will it be one rule today and another tomorrow. But there will be one law, eternal and unchangeable, binding at all times upon all peoples; and there will be, as it were, one common master and ruler of men, named God, who is the author of this law, its interpreter, and its sponsor."[24] The best political practices are transferable to other cultures and vice-versa. Failing this test, policies should not be considered inviolable.

4. *Also present in this model is a collective* (Gen. 47:13-27). While one may be justifiably suspicious of collectivized approaches to the economy, especially in light of the rise and fall of empires in this century, nonetheless, the role of the collective in preserving the grain is illustrated here—at least as a temporary measure. It should also be noted that this centralized plan is concerned with necessities, not "wants."

Again, one must be careful not to overreact against the excesses of recent times. Even if the majority of cases of collectivism are disastrous, one cannot on scriptural grounds rule out an exceptional or limited use of collectivist models as warranted by emergencies. It is the case, however, that such collectivist approaches are condoned only if they match conditions similar to this episode.

There is a significant difference between statist collectives and private cooperatives. Private charities have long known of economies of scale, and it is merely a wise use of resources to eliminate multiple agencies that perpetuate their own inefficiencies. One of the surest tests of the legitimacy of centralization is whether or not it is truly

---

[24] Cicero, *On the Commonwealth* (Indianapolis: Bobbs-Merrill, 1929), 216.

economical. If a task may be done more quickly or effectively by centralizing without violating any other ordained sphere, such economy is hard to fault. On the other hand, if centralization squelches humanity or violates other valid provisions, then it should be eschewed. While it would be unwise to construct the charter for a state on this model alone, yet, there may be some limited use of a co-operative in a godly model.

In the first phase of saving, Joseph used a 20% taxation rate. Later, when the famine was in full-force, Joseph received money in exchange for these crops. One may question whether or not he should have received profit from what already belonged to the people. However, there is no evidence of protest from the people about this matter. They seemed willing to pay for the crops, when the other surrounding groups were starving. The people were paying for Joseph's industry and wise pre-planning. Twenty per cent was fair in this situation. When their money was used up, they sold their livestock and eventually pledged themselves to be Pharaoh's servants. From that time on, a 20% rate—the maximum tax rate recorded in Scripture (and that during an international emergency)—was established for whatever produce was grown (Gen. 47:26). The only tax-exemption was for the priests and their lands (Gen. 47:22, 26), a basis for tax exemption for religious charities and their essential properties.

Profit and acquisition are also present in this episode (cf. also Ex. 3:22); and this is not merely another scheme for redistribution of wealth. Joseph made a profit, and he even traded the commodity for profit, the acquisition of land, and indentured servanthood. State policies do well not to condemn the profit motive or the acquisition of personal property. All it should avoid is the unjust acquisition of such (e.g., Mk. 4:19).

On Maturity of Character (Abraham, Esau, Jacob, Joseph)

Joseph is elevated in three stages: first as the household chief in Potiphar's house; then as the deputy to the prison chief; and finally, as Pharaoh's top assistant. Eventually, he would be bowed down to (as his dreams originally expressed) by his ten brothers (chapter 42), then by the addition of the 11th brother (chapter 43), and ultimately by his entire family (chapter 46).

Joseph is a prime example of growth in maturity. Joseph is first introduced at the age of 17. He was selected by God for a prime role, but was a bit proud of his status. An experience with being trafficked, a false accusation, and at least two years in jail took a good bit of his pride away. Joseph is maturing in character and, by the age of 30, he assumes one of the most important roles in the world at that time. He will continue to mature and in the coming chapters, he is depicted as wise, forgiving, faithful, and respected. The working of the Holy Spirit does bring maturity.

Other characters had similar trajectories. The patriarch Abraham, for example, showed some character defects when he tried to pass his wife off as his sister and when he deferred to his wife and produced a son with Hagar. Abraham, at the end of his life, was a very admirable man. Yet, his spiritual path was not always straight up. Over his long life, he grew as an exemplar of faith. Hebrews chapter 11 devotes much praise for him.

Jacob (and even Esau also) grew in their character from some of their low points as youth. Jacob started off as a bit spoiled and a momma's boy, who was also an opportunist. He met the Lord through several night encounters, which made lasting impressions on his godliness. It is a tribute to the Holy Spirit that these patriarchs exhibit the trajectory of sanctification. Despite their weaknesses, foibles, deceit, or scandals, the Lord still used them—and uses people like that today.

Joseph's Pranking; Joseph's Provision (Genesis 42-44)

Jacob opens Genesis 42 with a rebuke of his sons for not showing proper initiative. He asks why they are standing around when distant grain may be found in Egypt. He then deputizes his sons to travel to Egypt and bring back enough grain to survive the famine.

Ten (of the original 12) sons travel as a party to Egypt. Jacob still grieves the loss of Joseph and keeps young Benjamin home with him so that he will not lose another son. This, too, will become part of the drama in this narrative.

As the party arrives in Egypt, they unknowingly meet their estranged brother, Joseph. From the chronology above, it is now at least 20 years since they had last seen young Joseph. More of his life had been lived by this time away from his family than with his family. His physique was different, his high position of authority would have been totally unexpected, and in every way, he seemed to be an acculturated Egyptian. He had an Egyptian wife, Egyptian servants, spoke Egyptian, and was ensconced in the highest echelon of Egyptian pattern. It will be some time before they realize this is Joseph.

Notwithstanding, he quickly recognizes them and is moved to tears in these chapters as he realizes this.

There are three visits from Joseph's Canaan-based family to Egypt. The first of those is in chapter 42. The predicament is described, and the entourage journeys to Egypt in search of grain. When they arrive, Joseph quickly identifies them. He accuses them of spying or seeking to uncover the weaknesses of Egypt. The brothers, of course, deny this. They maintain that they are simply seeking to provide for their family during the famine. However, Joseph reiterates his accusation and imprisons them (42:13-14).

As the narrative continues in Genesis 42:13-20, Joseph imprisons his brothers. He then exacts a steep price for freedom—requiring that the brothers return and bring back young Benjamin to prove that they are not spies or dishonest. While they are in jail, their guilt for prior acts rises to the surface. They grieve—over 20 years after the fact—over how they mistreated their little brother, Joseph. They believe (almost Karma-like) that God is now judging them for those misdeeds. Their guilt (42:21-26) is becoming undeniable (for other *examples of guilt in these chapters, cf. 42:13-15; 43:17-18*).

They have no choice but to cooperate with Joseph. As they return, extra silver (42:27-34) is placed in their sacks along with the grain from Egypt's storehouses. They rightly fear that they might be charged for theft but continue onward to give this sad report to Jacob. When Jacob learns what has happened (vss 35-38), he is distraught and ready to die.

Worth noting, several references are made to God in this passage. The following provide glimpses into the character of God, known at this time:

> 42:18, 28 (God is to be feared; and God is in control of events.)
> 43:14. 23, 29 (God is almighty, gracious, and covenantal.)

It is also worth noting how frequently Joseph is moved to compassion. He is not focused on vengeance nor on gaining benefit from all this. Joseph wept at several points in these passages: 42:24, 43:30, 45:2, 14-15. Like our Lord, he was moved to compassion as he observed the effects of sin in this family and in our world.

Genesis 43 records the second visit to Egypt by this family. Jacob had earlier pledged that he would never allow any of his sons to return to Egypt. He did not want to risk losing more. He'd already lost Joseph, now Simeon was held hostage, and he certainly did not wish to lose Benjamin.

Nevertheless, the famine continues, Jacob reconsiders (43:1-14), and he sends another entourage to Egypt. Judah vouches that he will make sure they do not lose Benjamin to these Egyptian pirates. He pledges that he will be personally responsible for the younger brother (43:9). As the first instance in the Bible of one voluntarily offering his life for another, Judah pledges his life for the security of Benjamin (and the family).

Jacob then gathers a large peace offering, consisting of spices, nuts, and silver to take to pay Pharaoh. In fact, he provides twice the amount of silver (v. 12) that was returned in the mouth of the sacks, so that they could not be accused of theft. He prays for God Almighty (*El Shaddai*) to have mercy on their mission and sends them on their way.

When the troupe arrives, Joseph prepares a large feast in his own home (43:15-24) for the traveling brothers. As Joseph shows great hospitality (v. 16), like the father in the Prodigal Son parable who kills a fattened calf to celebrate, the brothers can only project that he is trying to set them up to kill or enslave them. They explain to the chief steward that they found silver in their sacks on their first return, that they did not steal it, and that they had brought back double to repay. They were assured that "your God, the God of your father" had done this and advised not to fear.

As the feast progressed, Joseph arrives and is given the gifts. He enquires about their aged father, but the brothers do not detect his interest. Joseph then spies Benjamin, and he dissolves into emotion. He must excuse himself (v. 30) and secludes himself in a place to weep. He returns after washing his face, and serves the brothers a lavish meal. Interestingly, Benjamin receives a serving that is five times the size of the others (v. 34).

Joseph is clearly toying with these brothers. He puts them through some agony, while the Lord wanted them all to learn about his providence.

What Joseph learned at the hands of his brothers, he is now teaching decades later: that God is sovereign even over acts of deception and depravity.

Providence Continued (Genesis 43-44)

If this were a classic drama, each act would further reveal the providence of God. Could you keep a journal of the "accidents" in these chapters? A journal or drama script would actually show providence, not accidents. In a famous sermon, R. C. Sproul recounted the various turning points of the plot in these chapters, commenting insincerely at each division: "And this all happened by accident." The cumulative effect is unforgettable. Below is a summary of these chapters (since some episodes have already been discussed above) if they were a play script, divided into Acts and Scenes.

Act 1: The First Visit to Egypt: Arrival and incarceration of the hungry entourage

Scene 1: Accusation of espionage (42:1-12)
Scene 2: Digging deeper into the family background (42:13-17)
Scene 3: On Day 3, the price of freedom—and a slip: "I fear God" (42:18-20)
Scene 4: Guilt, Self-Righteousness, and Compassion (42:21-24)

Act 2: The First Return and Reaction of Jacob

Scene 1: Governor Joseph sets up their return (42:25-26)
Scene 2: The brothers discover illicit silver (42:27-28)
Scene 3: Reporting to Father Jacob (42:29-35)
Scene 4: Jacob's anguish and rejection of collateralizing Benjamin (42:36-38)

> Jacob in his old age bears characteristics we are accustomed to associate with the very elderly. He dominates the family, sees issues in stark terms of black and white, and makes assertions which express is own passionate feelings; but everyone knows that he will have to go back on what he categorically stated. He could afford to refuse Reuben's offer because it was made at a time when there was food in store, but continuing shortage of rain forces the family to live on its stocks, until the situation was again becoming desperate. (J. Baldwin, 184)

Act 3: The Second Visit to Egypt

Scene 1: Jacob relents, Judah's surety and Benjamin as collateral (43:1-14)

Scene 2: Joseph throws a lavish feast—or is it a trick? (43:15-25)

Scene 3: Governor Joseph converses about the entourage's father (43:26-34); and exhibits considerable *pathos* (30-31)!

Act 4: The Second Return to Canaan

Scene 1: Governor Joseph sets up their second return—this time with a charge (44:1-9)

Scene 2: Process of elimination (or Providence?) (44:10-13) to ascertain the villian

Scene 3: Back at the palace: true repentance and atonement (44:14-34); Judah's long speech

Act 5: First Revelation of Joseph (45:1-8).

The applications are numerous. We see the following:

1. Guilt. The brothers are truly having to face up to their sin. They had virtually murdered Joseph and sold him into slavery. Sure, he was a bit obnoxious, but their mistreatment of him was not justified.
2. Compassion. We also see the tenderness of Joseph. Rather than seeking to exact an eye for an eye, he is often moved deeply and truly loves (and forgives) his brothers.
3. Repentance. As true guilt mounts, these brothers are gradually being brought to true repentance. It may arrive only in stages, but eventually they will not offer any excuses. They have resisted

admitting their guilt for over two decades, but God is leading them to repentance, which foregoes any excuses.
4. Atonement. Judah offering his life in place of another, if he cannot return his hostage brother, is bold and unusual.
5. Reconciliation. We are given a beautiful OT portrait of forgiveness and reconciliation. Once guilt is confessed and forgiveness occurs, there is true reconnection of affection.
6. Providence is surely the major message. God's invisible hand is at work. Jesus would later confirm that not a sparrow falls without our Father knowing it; also the hairs on our heads are numbered (cf. Mt. 10:29-31).

As such, even when people mean things for ill, God may structure those to good.

No Longer Concealed: God's Purpose Now Revealed (Genesis 45)

Chapter 45 of Genesis may be outlined as follows:
1. A stunning revelation — 45:1-4
2. A gracious consolation — 45:5-7
3. The explanation to take home to Jacob — 45:8-13
4. Weeping and hugging — 45:14-15
5. A minor theme: Note the witness to the Egyptians; their responses (in v. 2 and vss 16-20)
6. Joseph's bounty — 45:21-24 (and his counsel, knowing them [23])
7. Jacob relieved — 45:25-28

In these chapters, we see "the certainty that God's will (not man's) was the controlling agent shining out in every event." (Kidner, 206). This is "applied theology." (Kidner) The chapters in this Joseph cycle are pointing to the resolution that is so clear in the chapter. The buildup is strong; the climax beautiful.

Joyce Baldwin notes: "The life of Joseph so perfectly illustrates the overruling providence of God that it is important to consider its relevance for ourselves and the troubles we encounter in our lives." Ultimately, Joseph saw that he'd not be forsaken by God. "In a mysterious way God had made use of the ill will of his brothers to achieve their rescue in time of famine." (Baldwin, 190)

Derek Kidner (209) provides some explanation on the number of relatives who went down (cf. Gen. 46:20 w Acts 7:14): A total of 70 is listed (acc to the subtotals in vss. 15, 18, 22, 25). But Dinah should be added (71), But subtract Er, Onan, Joseph, Manasseh, Ephraim (v. 20) as already in Egypt for 66 persons. Then v. 27 adds back Joseph's two sons, Joseph, and Jacob himself to total 70.

These chapters cry out with a question: in what conditions does God's sovereignty NOT work? After reading these, can one honestly say that God's sovereignty cannot work in these areas?

1. Family dysfunction and jealousy?
2. An innocent victim thrown into terrible physical conditions?
3. Slavery and human trafficking?
4. A dramatic rise to responsibility (as in Potiphar's estate)?
5. Accusations of rape or sexual impropriety?
6. Imprisonment?
7. Fat years and lean years (famine): all economic cycles?
8. Sibling rivalry and dishonesty?
9. Serving in a pagan administration?[25]
10. Distrust by guilty brothers?
11. Family concerns?   Other?

One may line up all the disasters, deceptions, depravities, or scandals and scoundrels, but none of these thwart or stop the sovereign actions of God who is over all. Indeed, the book of Genesis seems to wish to portray all of these as proofs that no conditions defeat our Sovereign.

By surveying these conditions of affliction, duress, and suffering, it becomes clear when the NT will later assert that, whether the condition is famine, poverty war, or death, God does not desert his people. Moreover, nothing in all of creation can separate us from the love of Christ. It is helpful to compare the words in Romans 8:35-39 to these chapters in which God so manifestly provides for Joseph—and the line that will lead to Jesus, the Messiah.

---

[25] Proverbs 16:7 KJV "When a man's ways please the Lord, he makes even his enemies to be at peace with him."

A Family Reunion and Resettlement (Genesis 45-46)

After Joseph has revealed his true identity—along with crediting God for engineering all things—his family is astonished. He cautions his family not to be distressed nor angry with themselves (Ge. 45:5). He notes emphatically that God was working in all these details and sent him ahead "to preserve for you a remnant on earth and to save your lives by a great deliverance." (45:5, 7)

He puts these family members in their place, telling them that contrary to appearances, "it was not you who sent me here, but God" (v8). That is the key to reconciling oneself to adverse dynamics, family or otherwise. He then sends them back to explain things to his father, wanting Jacob to be comforted and to know that God is working all things out.

As he finishes this explanation, he dissolves into tears and embraces Benjamin, his brother. It is quite an emotional scene, if properly understood. In addition, the Egyptians learn about this turn of events and give Joseph's family the blessings of livestock, carts to carry back the booty, and precious commodities. The Egyptian bounty also includes elaborate gifts for Jacob, Joseph's father. (45:16-24)

The advance party reaches Jacob, who cannot believe their message. It had been too long, the years had been too cruel. However, as the gifts begin to roll in on many carts, Jacob finally believes the wonderful story and is relieved (45:25-28). At last, Jacob is convinced and agrees to go and meet Joseph in Egypt.

En route to Egypt, Jacob offers a sacrifice at Beersheba, and God once again speaks to him (addressing him doubly, "Jacob! Jacob?"). The Lord reassures Jacob that it is safe to go down to Egypt and that the Lord with remain with him and bring him home. The assurance is concretized as: "And Joseph's own hand will close your eyes." (Gen. 46:4) Genesis 46:3-4 is one of four "do not fear" narratives (cf. also 15:1, 21:17, and 26:24), which are founded upon the sovereign kindness of God.

All of Jacob's/Israel's sons who go down to Egypt are listed for posterity in Genesis 46:8-27. The number of 70 in this family will serve as a massive population nucleus. F. F. Bruce explains the NT Commentary from Stephen' speech in Acts 7 (*Acts*, 148): "In Gen. 46:27 and Ex 1:5, the LXX** has "seventy-five" for the MT "seventy." The MT total includes Jacob, Joseph, and Joseph's two son; the LCC reckoning omits Jacob and Joseph, but includes nine sons of Joseph. Josephus follows the Hebrew text." Both readings were known by the first century (e. g., Philo).

** The LXX of Gen. 46:27 reads: "And all the souls who came with Jacob into Egypt, who issued from his loins, apart from the wives of the sons of Jacob, were sixty-six persons. And the sons of Jacob who were born in Egypt were nine persons. All the souls of the house of Jacob who entered Egypt were seventy-five." [Note: these additional ones were likely younger sons of Manasseh and Ephraim (already in Egypt) or Egypt born sons of Joseph.]

Jacob comes full circle in Genesis 46. God appears to him at Beersheba. Remember the Lord met him earlier at Bethel. Jacob has come to know God as the appearing God.

Jacob's reception in Egypt and settlement is detailed at the end of Genesis 46 (vss 28-34). He and his family arrive at the predetermined area of Goshen, and Joseph smothers his father with tears and affection. Jacob feels his life may safely end, so great is this reconciliation. Joseph will also further pave the way for his father before his meets Pharaoh.

This is a new beginning for the patriarch. He had left his home (as had Abraham) and follows God.

"A father on his way to see his son pauses to worship the God of his own father." Back in Genesis 26:23-25, God had appeared to Isaac. Isaac built an altar there, "and a generation later his son offered sacrifices at that place." (Hamilton, 589)

The God of these patriarchs is reliable in his promises. Sometimes, they may take longer than expected to arrive, but God is as sovereign for Joseph and Jacob, as he was for Abraham and Isaac. He is, indeed, the same "yesterday, today, and forever."

Preparing for Famine . . . and Exodus: Pharaoh and Joseph's Family: (Genesis 46b-47)

The context of the next stage of God's redeeming work begins in the closing verses of Genesis 46. There we find Joseph the insider preparing his family to meet Pharaoh. While an eye that has not been informed of these earlier chapters might be blind to the secret workings of God, Joseph lays the groundwork for his family to succeed in Egypt. It is not, of course, to be taken for granted that Egypt would facilely allow a foreign cell to reside in its boundaries. However, *"When a man's ways please the Lord, he makes even his enemies to be at peace with him."* (Proverbs 16:7)

Joseph explains to Jacob what he should say to Pharaoh. First, Joseph will report to Pharaoh, who will naturally inquire about Jacob's line of work. The experienced son tells his father to answer that Jacob's family are shepherds, who are accustomed to caring for livestock. This would be no threat to the powerful Egyptian king. Joseph also advises his father to identify himself as a "servant" to Pharaoh. Thus, he would not be threatening in any fashion.

The King of Egypt and Governor Joseph's father then meet face-to-face in Genesis 47:1-10. Minding the finest court protocol, Joseph presents five of his brothers, and introduces these "servants" as simple shepherds. They request, as already arranged, to be allowed to live in Goshen, to which Pharaoh generously agrees. Pharaoh even extends an invitation to any of Joseph's brothers to care for his own livestock (v. 6).

Finally, the patriarchs meet. Pharaoh inquires to his age, and Jacob replies that he is 130. It has been a long time, since he (and his mom) cheated Isaac out of his blessing. God has been with Israel all the time, and now in a surprise, Jacob blessed Pharaoh. One would expect the opposite, namely, for the most powerful man in the world to bless the humble shepherd. Joseph is apparently permitted to grant real estate licenses, and gives property in Goshen to Jacob's flock (certainly with Pharaoh's blessing).

After Jacob settles in Goshen, the brunt of famine hits (47:13-22). There was no food, although Joseph had wisely stored supplies. As the famine takes its toll, Joseph becomes Pharaoh's Overlord, now selling the stored grain back to the people. Those profits were, then, given to Pharaoh (47:14). Similarly, when that supply was exhausted, Joseph collected livestock (v. 16) in place of money for food, giving that to Pharaoh. This was, of course, a gradual enslavement and thorough governmental confiscation, considering the people had originally contributed to pre-saved supplies.

Later, all money and livestock supplies were possessed by Pharaoh, so the people sold their fields and land in exchange for food. Finally, the people became indentured servants (v. 21) in exchange for food. Wise Joseph gave them seed for planting—the famine conditions now abated—and required them to return 20% of their harvest to Pharaoh. The people agreed, Pharaoh was enriched, and Joseph's reputation among governors continued to soar.

Surprisingly, the people were grateful for this, praising Joseph for saving their lives and requesting continued favor in his eyes. (v. 25) Moreover, the Israelites were also being blessed, as they settled in Goshen and acquired property there. Their population grew, as did their prosperity. Such increase would later lead the Pharaohs of the Exodus period to fear the prowess and prosperity of Israel.

Jacob would live in Goshen an additional 17 years (Gen. 47:28), dying at the age of 147. When it was time for his passing, he summoned Joseph and requested that he not bury his body in Egypt. He was a citizen of God's Canaan and wished to be buried with his people. He made Joseph covenant by oath to take his bones out of Egypt, as he died. This hope and trust in God's promise is the last signature of Jacob's life. With frailty of body, he leaned on his walker and worshiped; with vitality of spirit, he looked for the promised land.

Remembering Joseph's earliest dreams may remind us that God revealed what would happen to young Joseph all along. It would be wrong to infer that God was either surprised by all the twists and turns in this plot or that he is unable to write the plot. Rather, he is governing, while Joseph governs on a much smaller (but still pretty impressive) scale. Can't God use the message, even with an imperfect messenger? He certainly did in these chapters of early history.

Hebrews 11:21-22 provides a suitable NT epilogue, stressing the active faith of Jacob: "By faith Jacob, when he was dying, blessed each of Joseph's sons and worshiped as he leaned on top of this staff. By faith Joseph, when his end was near, spoke about the exodus of the Israelites from Egypt and gave instructions about his bones." Such faith, especially noting the patriarch's imperfections as a young man, is the sustaining fuel over generations.

Providence Through and Through (Genesis 47-48)

Providence is defined in the Heidelberg Catechism (#27-28) as: *"The almighty and everywhere present power of God; whereby, as it were by His hand, He upholds and governs heaven, earth, and all creatures; so that herbs and grass, rain and drought, fruitful and barren years, meat and drink, health and sickness, riches and poverty, yea, and all things come, not by chance, but by His fatherly hand.* (Question #27; Cf. Acts 17:26-27).

Question 28, then, adds: "What advantage is it to us to know that God has created, and by His providence doth still uphold all things? *Answer: That we may be patient in adversity; thankful in prosperity; and that in all things, which may hereafter befall us, we place our firm trust in our faithful God and Father, that nothing shall separate us from His love; since all creatures are so in His hand, that without His will they cannot so much as move."*

Providence is seen in these chapters in many ways, as listed below.

1. The mercy of providence seen in the agreeableness of Pharaoh (vs 1-6).

Ligon Duncan comments on this response of Pharaoh: "Humanly speaking, we wouldn't have expected a warm reception for Jacob's family. But mere man isn't in control here, and even Pharaoh, considered a god by his own people, is not in control. It is the God of Abraham, Isaac, and Jacob who is in control." It is noted that this passage shows how God cares for us, even if not immediately. Duncan continues: "We know that because we do the right thing doesn't result automatically in our temporal happiness and peace. There are in fact occasions in our lives when doing the right thing provokes the evil one, or provokes the professing church or the world against us. Christians keep the Lord's Day and then they get the sack, or they don't get promotion, but here in this passage we see that in God's goodness he rewards the faith of Jacob. Think of the tremendous thing that Jacob has done. He has uprooted himself from the land of promise. He has committed himself to dying in a strange land, a pagan land; He'll never again see the land of his fathers with his own eyes, and God rewards his faith that obeys God with these kind providences, a splendid fertile and peaceful land for his family to settle into. God confirms that his hand is upon Jacob's family."

2. Next, the blessing of the God of providence rests on Jacob (vss 7-10). The differences between Pharaoh and Jacob are displayed clearly here. Those stark contrasts are between: a Jew and a Gentile; a commoner and a king; the humble head of a family destined to become a mighty nation, and a mighty monarch of a people soon to be humbled; a herdsman and one who abominated herdsmen; an older man dressed as a shepherd and a younger man dressed in royal apparel. Nonetheless, God's sovereign providence applies to each.

3. The kindness of providence is seen in Pharaoh's generosity to Joseph. The powerful king of Egypt remains very grateful to Joseph. He spares no expense in helping him reunite with his family. God's kind providence best explains a secular ruler showing such kindness.

4. The provision of providences spares Joseph and his family during the severe famine (vss 13 ff). During this season, Joseph is quite the trader. He is routinely enhancing the assets that God has already provided. During these famine years, Joseph trades up from his beginning assets to receive:

    a. Money for food;
    b. Herds for grain;
    c. Lands and voluntary slavery for life.

Geoff Thomas comments: "You might not have noticed that there is no mention of the name of God in this chapter. The focus is on Joseph. God seems out of the picture altogether. But he's not; it is all about the providence of God. Though hidden, he is, through Joseph, working his purposes out. Secular historians have a term, 'methodological atheism,' because all they can see are men and movements. They mistake the hiddenness of God for the absence of God. The Bible never does."

So Joseph saved not only his family but the Egyptians and that was a clear fulfillment of God's promise to Abraham, "*I will bless those who bless you . . . and in you all the families of the earth shall be blessed*" (Gen.12:3). He kept alive the nation and so he kept alive the seed of the woman the line of Abraham and so Christ came in the fulness of time.

5. Providence kept Jacob trusting in God until the end (28-31). Once God began to care for Jacob, he was kept til the end. That calls for us to view ourselves as people who are pilgrims—not always settled as citizens of this world.

Our calling as pilgrims is to set our hope on that heavenly city which has true and eternal foundations. That is the destination of all the saints. Is that the focus of your discipleship? Is your hope there rather than here? Is your hope in the fulfillment of God's plan for all his people? Or are you wrapped up in smaller things? Jacob, here, sets an example for us. For those of us who are pilgrims in a strange land, our sight must be on that city with foundations, and our hope must be in the promise of God, and nothing else. If our sights are off, and our hope is off, we are simply not pilgrims. We're just not disciples of the same God who is the God of Jacob. May God enable us to be pilgrims despite all the enticements of the world, and set our hope on that place which is to come and to trust in his promises more than all the earthly blessings which we could possibly obtain.

Of course, God's providence is taught all throughout the OT. It is clearly exhibited in: 1 Kgs 22:19-36; Dan. 4:34-35; Ps. 135:6, 33:10-11.

Providence is explained in the Westminster Confession of Faith (5:1) in these words: "God the great Creator of all things does uphold, direct, dispose, and govern all creatures, actions, and things, (Dan. 4:34–35, Ps. 135:6, Acts 17:25–26) from the greatest even to the least, (Mt. 10:29–31) by his most wise and holy providence, (Prov. 15:3, Ps. 104:24, 145:17) according to his infallible foreknowledge, (Acts 15:18, Ps. 94:8–11) and the free and immutable counsel of his own will, (Eph. 1:11) to the praise of the glory of his wisdom, power, justice, goodness, and mercy. (Is. 63:14, Eph. 3:10, Rom. 9:17, Gen. 45:7, Ps. 145:7).

The Sovereign's providence is not limited by sinful subjects.

Blessings and AntiBlessings (Genesis 48-49)

Genesis 48-49 details the blessing of the next generation. One wonders is these blessings predict irony or destiny?

Before he died, Jacob achieved this purpose of elevating Joseph in this unusual way, by adopting both of Joseph's sons as his own, on a par with Reuben and Simeon (verse 5). Each son of Joseph would receive one portion, and in doing so Joseph would receive a double portion compared to his brothers: as Jacob says to Joseph at the end of the chapter; *"And I give you one portion more than your brothers, which I took from the hand of the Amorite with my sword and my bow"* (v.22).

Jacob is near the end of his life. He has become a serious "blesser," having previously blessed Pharaoh (47:10), Joseph (48:15-16), and Ephraim and Manasseh (48:17-22). In chapter 49, he will issue blessings for his 12 sons. And some of those awards will be blessings and most will be anti-blessings—irony is mixed with destiny.

"The power of blessing and divine pronouncement has shaped the Genesis narrative," observed Bruce Waltke, who sees Jacob's life commencing and ceasing with inspired prophecies. "An oracle announced his destiny," wrote Waltke, "and now he announces the future of his descendants. Unlike Isaac, who transferred the divine blessing behind closed doors, creating rivalry and conniving between parents and siblings, Jacob gives his blessing openly, summoning all his sons to gather around. The narrative of Genesis, which began with God's blessing of creation, now ends with Jacob conveying divine blessing on his children." Genesis, which began with God's creation by speaking concludes with spoken blessings by a patriarch." (Waltke, 604)

Jacob assembles the lads for their farewell blessings (Rev. 7:5-8 presents the tribes similarly, with a slight variation). These predictions were as much about the development of a tribe as they were personal gifts. These are not merely personal blessings—they apply to the development of a people over time. This provides a "glimpse of the embryonic nation." (Cf. Dt. 33)

Following the introduction (vss 1-2), the sons are blessed in order of their birth mothers. First to be blessed are Leah's sons (cf. Gen. 35:23-26) in vss 3-5. After that will be Bilhah's and Zilpah's sons in vss 16-21, concluding with Rachel's two sons in vss 22-27.

Reuben is first blessed with an award that begins very positively. The lads were expecting positive blessings, and this was begun by praising Reuben for his honor, power, and being the first sign of Jacob's fecundity. However, the blessing turns sharply in v. 4, as it castigates Reuben as "turbulent," and no longer excelling since he had sex with Jacob's wife (Gen. 35:22). Reuben would go away largely disappointed with this blessing.

The next two awarded were Simeon and Levi (vss. 5-7). They were cited for their violence and vengeful slaughter of the people of Shechem after they'd raped their sister, Dinah (cf. Gen 34). To be sure, that was a horrible act, but Jacob does not predict good for them since they acted in anger and violence; their people would be scattered—and the tribe of Levi (the priests) would not be awarded land in Joshua's time as Israel gained the land of Canaan.

Judah is given a very positive award (49:8-12), but Zebulun's was somewhat positive, while Issachar's was negative. Issachar (49:14-15) was described as a lean donkey—not exactly associated with majesty or intelligence. He would settle in a pleasant land but eventually be pressed into slavery. And Zebulun was awarded nice territory (v. 13) near the Mediterranean coast. Zebulun would become prosperous due to his proximity to trading and commerce. Few of these are blessed due to their strong character.

Of the first six sons, only Judah has a uniformly positive blessing. He is depicted as a young lion who would be a mighty warrior—his hand would be on the "neck of his enemies." He would conquer many, and his brothers would praise him. Still, the most positive thing about his blessing was the prediction that a ruler would come from his tribe (vss 10-12). This ruler would hold the symbol of reign—a scepter—which would remain his until one arrived who was the Messiah, to whom all nations owed obedience (cf. Ps. 2:9-12). This Messiah, a descendant of Judah, would rule with an iron rod. He would also assume his reign riding on a donkey (as Jesus entered Jerusalem on Palm Sunday). Judah's tribe would produce a Messiah whose garments would be washed n blood, signifying the atoning death of Jesus. This is the single totally positive blessing among the first half of the sons; similarly, Joseph will be the primary positively blessed son in the second half of these blessings.

Next come the awards for the sons of the concubines Bilhah and Zilpah.

- Dan is blessed for bringing justice (49:16-18), but his character is compared to a serpent by the roadside or a viper who bites the heels of horses, throwing riders to the ground.
- Gad will be known as a tribe who is often attacked by raiders (indicating poor defenses and planning), and as one who pursues them after the fact (49:19).
- Asher (49:20) will be known as a culinary leader.
- Naphtali (49:21) will be known for producing beautiful offspring.

Again, if the lads were expecting a monetary inheritance, or a few acres of land, or commendation of their character, this would not be a great day in their history.

Of Rachel's sons, Benjamin is praised slightly for his fighting ability, and only Joseph (49:22-26) is given a great blessing. Joseph is blessed, and all the brothers would have a hard time protesting his value—since he had spared the entire family from the famine.

"All the wonderful overruling of God seen in the life of Joseph up to this point is part of a total plan for blessing which will not be experienced by his successors. Ephraim and Manasseh inherited the most fertile areas of the land of Canaan and flourished accordingly, but by the time of Amos and Hosea self-indulgence had brought about the ruin of the tribes oof Joseph . . . The promise stood until its recipients rejected out of hand their father's God." (Baldwin, 213)

What "blessing" would you pass on to your children? Blessings in the NT: Luke 1:48

The Passing of Jacob is provided in Gen 49:29-33. There, he requests to be buried with his people.

The phrase "gathered to his people," used earlier of Abraham and Isaac (35:29) reveals a view of death early on in the OT that expects continued consciousness after physical life ceases. It is not so much the end of existence as a gathering for a new company, a heavenly one.

The End of the Beginning (Genesis 50)

This final chapter draws together threads that were woven years earlier and that extend generations later. They provide a sense of completion and fulfillment.

The death of Jacob is presented in Genesis 49:29-50:3. Abraham purchased burial plots, and his family's bodies would return to those tracts of land. It was important to dispose of human remains and not merely leave them to the elements. Joseph (after another very emotional display) directed that his father be embalmed. During the lengthy period of Egyptian embalming, plus another month, the Egyptians joined in for the mourning of the death of the savior of Egypt.

Joseph requested leave of Pharaoh to transport his father's body to be buried in Canaan. Pharaoh accommodated, and even sent an entourage of his own officials for a state funeral. Representatives of the court, the military, and of course Joseph's family went up for this burial. Along the way, at one stopping point, the procession stopped to allow for an extended period of lament. For seven days, the funeral party wept, and the display even impressed the local Canaanites.

Finally, Jacob's sons arrive at the Cave of Machpelah, where his body is laid to rest. This man who began under such a cloud of deception was given the most elaborate burial in the Old Testament.

Once more, however, before this book's close, we see Joseph's faith and assurance (Gen. 50:15-21). Following the interment of Jacob's body, once again the brothers wonder if Joseph may not seek retaliation—now that father is no longer around to referee. Exhibiting what psychologists call 'projection' (reading the actions of others as you might act), the brothers wonder if Joseph might secretly be holding a grudge (50:15).

They then resume their fictionalizing and send word to Joseph that their father had explicitly requested that he forgive their sins. They present this message as from dad's last will and testament, conveying it to Joseph as from his "servants." These brothers clearly could not accept or understand forgiveness.

Joseph, however, knew the power of forgiveness. He advised his brothers not to be afraid and explained that he did not stand in the place of God (v. 19). He returns to the theme of this final part of Genesis, stating: "You intended to harm me, but God intended it for good to accomplish what is not being done, the saving of many lives." Joseph had a firm grasp on this truth: God is sovereign, even over all the affairs of men. Not only had Joseph truly forgiven his brothers, but the basis of that was the bedrock platform of the sovereignty of God.

Can you see how these verses apply in your own life?

Joseph's death is then recorded after he blesses Ephraim's and Manasseh's children. He lived to the age of 110, and the little brother thrown into a well died a hero of Egypt. More importantly, he rescued Jacob's line which led to the Messiah, keeping it from being snuffed out during the famine.

His final request, which showed his great faith, was that his children would take his body with them when they were delivered from Egypt. Joseph knew that God's work was not finished and that he would take his people to the land of promise. Thus, he charged them to take his bones with them when they were liberated. The keeping of this promise is recorded later in Exodus 13:19 and Joshua 24:32. Joseph's faith was as strong as Abraham's; and it looked forward to a citizenship far above any earthly city or region, one that cannot be tarnished or destroyed.

Two places in the NT comment on this faith: Hebrews 11 and Acts 7. In Acts 7, Stephen's sermon before his martyrdom draws on Joseph a good deal. Indeed, that was the primary example of pleasing God, proclaimed by the first martyr (after Jesus) of the NT church.

I ask the kind reader who has reviewed this much to allow me just a few final conclusions.

Conclusions

1. These patriarchal narratives are epitomes of the gospels. God is the same. Man is the same. Sin is the same. Salvation is the same. The God of Abraham, Issac, Jacob, Joseph, Sarah, Rachel, and others is the same, unchanging God. This first book of the Bible is always relevant.
2. Go back to Genesis 37. Did these dreams come true or not? As imperfect as Joseph was then (and his whole family), God gave the blueprint for what would happen in these dreams. They did come true, and only a sovereign Guarantor could produce that.
3. God is depicted in three main roles in the book of Genesis: (a) Creator; (b) Covenant-Maker; and (c) Governor-Provider. He forms all the external world, and he also relates to his people as the God of the Covenant who provides.
4. In this last role, you can't "unsee" God's providence, once you see it. It is everywhere, and it gives us:
a. Comfort during trials;
b. Confidence for the future;
c. Consolation amidst suffering.

This is the enduring faith for all the saints (Jude 3).

Finally, the providence of God perpetuated the line of Abraham through the heroic and wise stewardship of Joseph. Without him, if some evil force could have eradicated him, Jesus' line might have been extinguished. Matthew 1-2 even ties Jesus' birth to this cycle. "Both Josephs receive revelation in dreams, and both go down to Egypt. Both are involved with a king (Pharaoh, Herod). Both are followed by children who are destined to be saviors and rescuers . . ." (Hamilton, 714)

God is the same yesterday, today, and forever. He still provides. He is ever sovereign, even amidst scurrilous scandals, salacious scandals, debilitating deception, and dire depravity.

God triumphs, and Joseph saw this well when he told his gun-shy brothers that even if they intended things for ill, God overcomes and works all things together for his own plan. One may rest in that.

Where Did All This Come From? How Sin Began and Continues (Genesis 3)

Puritan exemplar John Owen said, "The greatest evil in the world is sin, and the greatest sin was the first."[26]

From time to time, any sane person will ask a basic question: why do bad things happen? Why is there death and tragedy? No matter how much we might shelter ourselves and our families, we cannot avoid the reality of evil in this world. And since most of those tragedies are caused by other human beings, from time to time, we'll allow our minds to revolve around this question: what is the nature of man, and why does it tend toward evil? It is simple, and I believe demanding, to ask: why will 20 Islamic hijackers fly planes into buildings and kill over 3,000 people?

Many different religions and philosophies suggest many different answers. For example:

Islam's comment on evil is to express the bald fatalism, "It's just Allah's will." Of course, that religion itself sanctions some murder and violence under the rubric of *jihad*. Islam accepts evil and terrorism as part of the norm of life. Indeed, there is some reward in the afterlife if one martyrs himself.

Hinduism, the largest religion in the east, cannot explain evil either. In fact, Hinduism believes that anything bad is "all part of the great ONE." For the Hindu, good and bad are slightly blurred as all merges into the great union of body and soul.

---

[26] Cited by Mark Jones, *Knowing Sin* (p. 23). Moody Publishers. Kindle Edition.

Materialism is also insufficient as it deals with evil. It reduces things to the smallest physical quantities, and thus sees evil as merely the outworking of an electro-chemical synapse. It's chemistry not morality to the materialist.

Similarly, the **Atheist** doesn't really have a basis for condemning evil or murder. If God does not exist, then morality of any kind is little more than personal taste or preference.

Christian Science: It's all in your head; there is no sickness, defect, or flaw in reality. You just need to think right!!

All cults and false religions fall dramatically short of either explaining the origin of evil or of providing an ethical basis for knowing good from evil.

However, one of the fantastic things about the book of Genesis is that it can and does explain evil and sin. Why, here in the earliest narrative of Christianity, there is even a "tree of knowledge of good and evil." Still, even **Judaism**, at least in its modern incarnations, does not deal with or provide a remedy for evil and sin.

And this passage, which is exactly as true and unmythical as the previous and later chapters of the Bible, gives us a wonderful explanation. It also ends up explaining quite a few other things as well as pointing us to hope in Christ.

I want us to review first: (1) the fall into sin; and (2) the cover-up.

The Origin of Sin

At the end of Genesis chapter 1, we learn about how God created man, and how everything was VERY GOOD. There was no sin, no evil of any kind, no deficiency whatsoever in the entire creation at that time.

After the seventh day (the day of rest) is described in the first few verses of chapter 2, the remainder of chapter 2 focuses on man as the crown of God's creation. Both Adam and Eve were created and set in the garden before sin entered the world. When God brought Eve to Adam, there was no shame, no violence in the entire world, and there was no sin or curse. By the end of chapter 2 of Genesis, this condition prevailed: "And God saw it, and it was Very Good." All that God had made was excellent and beautiful. All was in accord with his grand plan for the universe.

That is vital to know as we review Genesis 3. In fact, hear the final vs. of chapter 2: "The man and his wife were both naked, and they felt no shame." *No shame, because no sin.* It will later help us appreciate a vital fact—about the Fall of Satan—if we first understand this.

Now let's turn our attention to the biblical account of the entrance of sin into the world, first noting:

A. The anatomy of sin; what is going on in vss. 1-7.

We see here, not only the historic fall of Adam, but a pattern for sin in many other instances. At the opening of chapter 3, we can see that sin has entered the world. It is no longer a world free from sin and deceit. For the serpent has been possessed by Satan, who had obviously fallen himself. That serpent, we're told, was "crafty." There was no craftiness or deceit before the Fall. Satan is malicious and ever-so subtle in his forms of attack. Even his approaches are filled with trickery, cunning, and malice. He attacks us where we are weakest. Count on that. "Strangely enough, Satan sometimes [successfully] tempts men with the very thing which you might suppose would never come upon them." (C. Spurgeon)

Satan had fallen, and now he attempts to recruit more people for his evil crusade. He stubbornly refuses to admit God's lordship and persists in leading an insurrection; he thinks, somehow, that he can topple God. In fact, he continued to think that until Good Friday and, yes, he still thinks he may yet win a come-from-behind victory. He uses, most likely, the very thing that led to his own fall. Think about that as we work through this.

Notice the first part of Satan's attack: he subtly, not even explicitly, but indirectly calls into question God's ability to communicate. Rarely does temptation come to us in the form of overt atheism. The Evil One is a far better Tempter than that. He knows that such blatant rebellion may be so shocking as to provoke resistance. Instead, he creeps up on us, using deceit and sneaky tactics. He is crafty, after all.

Rather than directly disputing God's Word, Satan initially tried a much subtler approach, seeking to get Eve to question. He asked, "Did God really say, 'you must not eat from any tree in the garden'?" Turn back to Gen. 2:16-17 to see exactly what God said after locating Adam in Eden. The quote is: "You are free to eat from any tree in the garden;

but you must not eat from the tree of the knowledge of good and evil, for when you eat of it you will surely die."

Now before looking at Eve's answer, consider this question: what *should* Eve have done? What would have been, in other words, a proper response to this subtle seduction?

What she should have done is said, "No." She should not have entertained any possibility that God was either wrong or that he had mis-communicated in any way. She should *not* have entered into a debate or carried on a conversation with Satan over this question. To do so, and if you respond to temptation like this it is the same with you, only opens a person up Satanic influence. Don't converse with Satan under any circumstances. Don't entertain your doubts long enough to allow the Original Liar to distort truth further. That is one of those things, and there are many, that cannot ever be good in any situation.

Instead, Eve tries to answer the Evil One on his own turf. She does not turn to Adam and ask his help, nor does she obey God. Instead, she decides that a little dialogue cannot hurt too much. In v. 2, she speaks back to the serpent. There, she repeats most of what God told her. But "most of what God told her" is not enough; nor is it on target. You may want to note from this that, in general, whenever we have a conversation with those who do not believe, once we move to their turf that is a home field advantage that won't quit!

Eve said, "We may eat from the trees in the garden, but God did say, you must not eat from the fruit from the tree that is in the middle of the garden, and you must not touch it, or you will die." Is that an exact quote of what God originally said? Learn how dangerous it can be to quote 90% of God's Word. People still do that often.

Compare what she said to the previous page (Gen. 2:16-17). It is ever so close, but it misses the mark at one place. *Eve ADDED to Scripture.* Now you might think that that is certainly better than taking away from it. To some it might seem that way, but if we know that God's revealed truth is perfect, then we know that it can be just as wrong to try to improve it as it is to try to minimize it. She added the phrase, "and you must not touch it." Why do you think she added that?

Probably out of good intentions. Again, good intentions cannot be the standard of Scripture. Eve probably thought that she was helping out God a little. Do you ever feel that you should do that? If so, you might recall this. Deep down on some subconscious level, she probably realized that she was in trouble. Satan's opening parry had caused more damage than one might think. If true, it undermined confidence in God. It called into question his ability to reveal. Either he could not reveal adequately to his creatures, or else he revealed but they could not understand him. Either would be fatal for our faith.

Rayburn comments: "When she adds 'must not touch it' it appears she has already accepted into her heart something of the serpent's attitude; she has begun to separate God's rights from her own; magnifying God's strictness, she seems open to the suggestion that his demands are unreasonable—she will have many successors!"

As Eve began to ponder that issue, she was probably scared, afraid that God's Word might not be as reliable as she once thought. So, out there alone, apart from her headship and engaged in a conversation that she never should be having, with a foe that was obviously her superior, she resorts to a form of humanism. She tried to add to God's Word, using her own strength and human ingenuity.

Then Satan counterattacks. He knows two things at this point: (1) somehow, he knows that Eve is on the ropes, much more so than one would think; and (2) he knows what really caused him to fall. With Eve in dangerous territory, the Father of Lies, knows how to plant one in the human heart. So, he goes deeper in his assault on God, and alleges, now with more frontal and direct contradiction, in 4-5: "You will not surely die. For God knows that when you eat of it your eyes will be opened, and you will be like God, knowing good and evil."

Now he has moved to defaming deity. First, he contradicts God's Word—be very wary of those who do that—he tells Eve that 'you will not surely die.' He blatantly opposes what God has said in Gen. 2:17. But he is not content to stop there in his temptation. He moves further in his attack to God's veracity and his ability at the same time.

To lead her astray—and he still works this way—Satan tries to get people to think of God as a small, ineffectual god. He said, "look, God didn't say such a thing. Or if he did, it is only because he is not a very comprehensive God. All that will happen if you disobey is this: God will be threatened because he is fairly small in his scope to affect change. God is really intimidated by humans, especially if they accumulate too much knowledge." What happens, according to

Satan—and many intellectual elitists—is that if you grow really wise, you can leave God behind and out of your life, and if you do that, you will almost become like him, knowing good and evil.

That, recall, was the only tree out of the entire creation that God told Eve not to take from. It helps sometimes, under temptation, to recall all the things God allows us to do; and it is only some few that he rules out.

Verse 6 reveals her thought process as she heads to sin. But the reality is that she has already fatally caved in. By letting Satan set the terms of the debate, Eve has given away the garden and doesn't even know it. She's on the ropes; it's like sending a kindergartner into a boxing ring against Mohammed Ali in his prime. There's no way she can win this battle. She does her best, but she should not have joined this conflict.

She is defeated and does not know it. Somewhere deep within herself, she has decided to taste the fruit. So, she rationalizes: that the fruit was "good for food and pleasing to the eye, and also desirable for gaining wisdom." But wait: where was there a shortage of food in the Garden of Eden? Had God not provided enough? Was there a threat of starvation?

Or what about her rationalization about, "pleasing to the eye?" Was the Garden of Eden ugly or lacking in aesthetic beauty? Hardly. What was really underneath was this: that it was "desirable for gaining wisdom." Ah, so she went for it, hook, line and sinker. Satan was right. He felled the human with the temptation that got him: there was some chance that man might be as smart as God. Oh, that is still a temptation in many ways today. Are not certain kinds of cloning eerily similar to this? Medical advance is one thing; the attempt to replicate human life might be stepping into God's territory.

The many ways that human beings set themselves up to equal God are all signs of sin.

Note that the record of the actual fall is very short, "and she took some and ate it." The root of sin is deep, you must know that, but its fruit is even longer. Rarely do we sin without some premeditation. Eve spent a long time considering what she was about to do; when she finally ate the fruit, the plunge did not take long.

But Eve did not act in obedience, and human history is irrevocably scarred from there on because of this sin.

She took the fruit and gave some to her husband, who joined in her complicity, and immediately the consequences started. Although they were the only two in existence, the shadow of guilt caused them to be ashamed and they realize that they were naked and exposed. The first thing they did after this sin was to attempt a cover-up.

But the consequences were just beginning. Note in the following verses both how they responded and also how this was the beginning of so many psychological maladies.

B. The pathology of sin (vss. 8-14); the second act]

Adam and Eve once had glorious and open fellowship with God. However, as soon as sin entered the world, their reactions changed. After the fall, when Adam and Eve heard God, they hid themselves from the Lord, trying to hide amongst the trees. But God asked, "where are you?" not in the sense that he was not omniscient but as a parent will ask a child, who has obviously sinned, "What have you done? God was seeking to arouse and convict Adam of sin; or perhaps he was summoning him to justice. Sometimes, if given the opportunity to repent, we will. Adam and Eve, however, did not.

In response, Adam answered, 'I heard you, I was afraid (partial truth), and I was naked so I hid.' Note the cover-up but also the genesis of fear. There was no fear heretofore; now Adam was afraid. Moreover, he is naked, and God asked him about that: "who told you that you were naked?" In other words, that was a new concept, and God asked about its source with Adam.

Then God asks Adam directly, "have you eaten from the tree?"

I find Adam's response here almost humorous, except it is still repeated so many times in our own homes to this day.

The BLAME GAME begins

First, Adam blames Eve; then he appeals to a higher court, blaming God! "The woman, the woman YOU put here, she gave me some and I ate." Any way of looking at it, Adam claimed to be a victim.

So, God moves on to the next person possibly responsible. Notice how quickly humans learn not to accept responsibility.

Second, God addresses Eve and asks her, "What is this you have done?" But it wasn't her fault, of course!! She pleads outright victimhood. "The serpent deceived me, and I ate." All she did, according to her confession, was "bite." The deception and the blame rested with the serpent.

God, then, goes to the *third* actor in this drama. When he approaches Satan, he does not ask questions; for he knows well the answers. God had already seen Satan's fall like lightning. To Satan, God begins to issue verdicts. The 'sentencing phase,' if you will, begins in Genesis 3:14. Thus far legal terminology, almost like that of a courtroom, had been used. God, the Judge, tries the case, acts in Infinite Fairness—as always—and convicts the sinners.

But be sure to notice this: Not only does death begin with this Fall, and all human sin, but also, the root of every psychological malady begins to bloom here. We see the first appearance of all of the ff: in this passage:

> Fear
> Shame
> Guilt
> Blame
> Deceit
> Death

Man falls, physically, spiritually, and psychologically. Every part of human nature is tainted henceforth. And all of the evil in the universe is traceable back to this.

Not a very good day, if those continue; and they do . . . far as the curse is found, far as the curse is found. Remember that when we sing the Christmas Carol. And the effects of the Fall are not erased nor diluted over time.

Pastor Rob Rayburn cites 17th century English Puritan John Howe:

"The stately ruins of this living temple still bear this doleful inscription over their portal -- here God once dwelt. Enough still appears of the admirable form and structure of the soul of man to show that the divine presence did sometimes reside in it: more than enough of vicious deformity to proclaim that he is now retired and gone. The altar is overturned and the candlestick is broken: and in place of the sacred incense, with its clouds of rich perfumes, there is a poisonous and hellish vapour continually rising up. . . . Behold the desolation! Behold the ruins of the fall! The faded glory, the darkness, the disorder, the impurity, the decayed state in all respects of this temple too plainly show that the great inhabitant is gone."

God, in the 3rd act of this drama, quickly pronounces a curse on each of the 3. Each curse is two-fold; physical and emotional.

First, to Satan, God pronounces that he will be:

    a. Cursed—crawl on belly

    b. enmity results between the offspring of Satan and the offspring of Woman

Next, to Eve (16), there will be:

    a. intense labor pain in childbirth.

    b. an emotional longing to control that will be frustrated.

Finally, to Adam

    a. The ground is cursed.

    b. Man will work in sweat and toil.

Each person had his chief interest cursed and the principle of frustration built into the fabric of life.

The Continued Operation of Sin follows these patterns of the Fall (James 1:12-14)

Now turn your attention to the NT to the first chapter of the epistle of James, v. 12. There, James resumes the theme of steadfastness under suffering. "Blessed," James says is the one who perseveres under trials. Not only are we to consider it pure joy, when we have various trials, but there is also a promised blessing. When we stand the tests of life, we receive a crown. It is easy to envision a college or high school graduate receiving his diploma at this time of year. That student has faced many tests. He is now graduating, and the diploma is a symbol of having passed all those tests. There is confidence in that, and God compares our passing tests to the trials of life. We are also assured by this passage that God loves us during these trials.

James then leads to the subject of temptation. This is something every Christian should know something about. We have trials of suffering that lead to perseverance; we also have trials over wisdom, knowing what to do. Some people have trials over their status in life.

But all of us have to learn how to deal with the trial of temptation. Verses 13-15 give us enduring perspective.

The first thing to note is: The believer cannot blame God for testing via temptation. Creatures, if allowed, will attempt to transfer their guilt to the Lord; they blame the Lord for their faults. But it is far better to confess sin than to try to pass it off.

Let me give examples of how some people try to pass sin off and blame it on God, borrowing from a Puritan (T. Manton, *in loc.*, 84-86)

- If they blame providence, the situation, the circumstances, or the mere placing of a trial before us.
- By attributing sin to the lack of grace or spiritual operation.
- All manners of claiming to be victims.
- When a person blames God, but all the while has nourished some sin.
- When a person has a defective understanding of how God's decrees work, as if they cause sin.

The human mind is most creative in its effort to transfer guilt from man to God.

Still temptation alone is not wrong for God to allow. If we understand this, facing trials will be a little bit better. No one should plead, "God is tempting me."

The reason is because God *allows* temptation, but he never seduces us toward sin. God also allows intermediating agents to tempt us, while he does not directly do the tempting. Certainly, he could prevent this from happening should he wish, but his plan also calls for tempting to test and strengthen us.

The passage continues to explain that God is not tempted by evil himself. He does not give Satan's sirens another thought. They have no impact on him. Our holy God cannot even look on evil, his eyes are so pure.

Neither does he do the tempting in any sin. Admittedly, some people get hung up at this point. We believe that God sovereignly rules over all and controls all. But that does not mean that he comes to the believer and directly tempts him. There is a difference between *allowing* and *causing* temptation. God does not, in that sense of causing, tempt anyone. Satan may, with God's permission, bring a host of temptations to us, but God himself does not participate. He does not, in other words, manipulate our arms, legs, or minds to run into sin.

So, remember, that God is removed from tempting us. Job is a classic illustration. In that book, Satan tried this theory out: people only believe because they've got it good. Strip away the blessings, and humans will curse God. That was Satan's recruiting scheme 4,000 years ago. God, of course, knew better.

So, God gave his approval to Satan to tempt one of the most blessed men around, Job. Satan and God entered into an agreement, in which God commanded that Satan not physically take the life of Job. All else was in play. And Satan gave Job his best, or worst as we might say. Job was fiercely tempted, and tempted by those closest to him to curse God. The whole time, God allowed Satan to tempt—but it was not God—and Job was faithful to the end. But God did not directly tempt him, he allowed others to do so, though. Thus, God is not faulted for the temptation. He never tries to knock the believer off the path of righteousness; that is the work of the devil. James makes that clear.

Verse 14, then, describes what really happens in sin. We have an anatomy of sin given to us in these vss (14-15). This being the pattern of nearly every sin, we ought to understand it. That is part of the wisdom God liberally gives.

A chain of events in time is detailed in those verses. James explains sin as happening in this fashion. It starts inwardly. It is ever so critical for you to know that sin is not merely an external act, nor a response of the flesh. It always starts internally. That clues us as to the nature of sin, and also about the target of salvation. The Book of Genesis tells us early on that "every inclination of the thoughts of man were only evil all the time." It is not only the final act that typifies sin, but the process leading up to it, beginning with our hearts.

We also learn that salvation is aimed out our hearts, not our bodies alone.

The PROCESS: Verse 14 describes where sin begins. It is hatched in "evil desire." The word (*epithumia*) is sometimes translated "lust," indicating that lust is not restricted to sexual activity alone. It also applies to anything that the flesh craves which God has not given. Sin begins with evil desire.

Every person is haunted by lust. It begins in our soul, which is like a sponge "always thirsting for something to fill itself. All of its actings . . . come out of some will and some desire. The will itself is bent toward lust, and sin Adam's Fall, people consult first with their desires." (Manton) Lust is the seed of sin.

The next step is that a person is "dragged away." Learn from this that if sin is not stopped and killed, it will continue to act. It is like those wildfires raging out west. They will not stop until they meet a more potent force. *Sin spreads; it is never in neutral.* Once sin is created in the human heart, it works on us and drags us away. The word picture is like a small piece of wood swept away by a roaring current.

When Ann and I were newlyweds, we went to see Amnicolola Falls in North Georgia. It was really quite a beautiful waterfall. After hiking up to the base of the falls, we allowed ourselves to be sprayed by the cascading waters, as a rainbow laced the falls on a beautiful spring day. Then we decided to hike the trail up to the top. After a brisk hike, when we arrived to the meadow at the top, I was amazed to see how small a trickle the beginning of that torrent was. What was huge and powerful at the base, was a small stream at one point at the top. We realized that, had we wished, we could have damned up that little stream with a few boards and there never would have been a waterfall. However, as the water rushed downward, it collected more volume and velocity. After collecting more water, and then dropping hundreds of feet, it exploded into a powerful waterfall.

What could have been stopped easily when it was a small trickle became unstoppable after a long period mirrored what sin is like. Sin, if stopped, is better stopped in its early stages. The sooner the thrust is blunted, the better. If you let sin rage for a long time, and pick up steam, it can become virtually impossible to stop. So, nip it in the bud. This passage tries to teach us not to be passive toward sin, but to be on guard.

James continues to depict the process. After temptation is sown amidst evil desire, the person becomes dragged away, and then is "enticed." The final word of v. 14 refers to a moral tipping point.

The next stage is that desire "conceives." After the seed grows for a while, it will come to fruition. It does not remain barren forever. When

sin is ripe, it conceives--much like a newborn is conceived after months of gestation--and it gives birth to sin. Sin finally occurs after:
> Temptation leads to evil desire
> Desire drags away
> Enticement nurtures the forming sin
> Sin is birthed, and finally it grows and leads to death.

This process agrees exactly with what Romans 6:23 teaches, "for the wages of sin is death." Once sin is conceived it takes on a life of its own. It becomes full-grown or mature, and it gives birth to death. That is how sin works. It does not fail to bloom and lead to death. God wants you to know something about this process so that you will nip it in the bud.

That is what happened in the first sin, in the Garden. Eve was initially tempted. She began to listen to Satan's evil promises. She mulled them over in her mind. Not having put those lies out of her mind, her temptation led to evil desire. She desired what Satan was offering: knowledge equal to that of God.

That desire began to drag her away. She was like an autumn leaf blowing down a whitewater river. The force of her urge began to quicken. Her rationalizations raced, justifying her action. She told herself that a little enlightenment couldn't be a bad thing. She gazed at the forbidden fruit, listening to Satan more than God. She was on the ropes, and justified the fruit as good for food and pleasing to the eye, when all along it was good for obtaining that knowledge which did not belong to her.

The enticement swelled within her. She began to look around and calculate what affect the sin might have, which was a sign that her mind has already fallen. She nurtured the forming sin, and did not put it to death. Once implanted, sin would lead to catastrophic and universal blossoms, but the mother of us all had already permitted the sin to grow within her.

Finally, she took the fruit and ate, and gave some to her husband. Sin was birthed, and it grew to death. Immediately after eating the fruit, their eyes were opened, sin reigned, and the entire universe came under the spell of death.

What started with something small grew into the greatest calamity in history. Death results from permitting temptation to grow. It will not go away without eradicating sin. We all have a little inheritance from Eve.

That is what happens in any other sin. Take, for example, divorce.

I have never known a couple to seek a divorce merely because of one tiff or a single temptation. It just doesn't happen instantaneously, even if movies show that. Rather, divorce is normally the death of a cherished relationship that arises after a long period of temptation. Here's how it normally works.

One spouse begins to believe he is not receiving all that he wants from the marriage. One thinks everyone else has a better, more jovial home and relationship. So, they begin to despise what God, in his providence, has given. Then, that tempted spouse begins to consider what she thought she never would. She wonders what a divorce would be like. That is the beginning of temptation. Temptation then, as James teaches, eventually leads to evil desire.

The next step in killing a marriage is that desire drags away. The spouse begins to look for other relationships. She allows herself more and more leeway in those once casual relationships. Her social life begins to soar. The more she allows temptation to drag her away the more potent the temptation becomes.

The person then begins to creep toward the edge of immorality. Like Eve, she thinks, "a little more fun; I deserve it. Everyone else does this," and a host of other rationalizations.

Then the tempted person, who is quite relishing in his decline, begins to set dates. Enticement nurtures the forming sin. There are many other intermediate steps before the murder of the marriage, but it is clearly on the brink. STOP, and if anyone here is close to this, please turn before too late!

Temptation grows and becomes embedded. It is tougher and tougher to shed, even if the tempted wanted to. Finally, an act is done, a marriage destroyed, a home and many other lives wrecked because this sin was not nipped in the bud. Sin is birthed, and finally it grows and leads to death. Marriages can die from sin just as surely as our bodies suffer physical death. It started small, perhaps even in playful innocence, but it was not snuffed out and led to death.

God wants us to understand this so that we avoid the deathtrap of sin. It is wisdom to learn this, that wisdom that James described, which comes from above and which God gives generously. Please take note of this.

A similar process takes place in any sin, ranging from fraud and slander to murder and rape. *The terminal act of sin is always an extension of inner lust.* God wants his children to know how to withstand temptation. He wants you to put this into practice this week.

And when you face it as a trial, when God is testing you, know this is how potent sin is. Commenting on James 4:16, Thomas Manton (1620–77) says, "First we practice sin, then defend it, then boast of it. Sin is first our burden, then our custom, then our delight, then our excellency." [cited in Mark Jones, *Knowing Sin* (pp. 45-46)].

Thus, we see the origin and continuing operation of sin. It is what is behind all the scandals, scoundrels, deception, and depravity in exhibited in the first book of the Bible.

Two final comments are in order as we close this small work. First, not only does sin work itself out in Genesis but it is woven all throughout the Bible. This dolorous plotline is far from contained.

Second, however, the Lord used and continues to use imperfect people. He is not such a weak God as to only be able to work, conditioned on having a winning team

Epilogue

Toward the latter part of the NT, Hebrew 11 contains a list of heroes of the OT. Many of these referred to above make this Hall of Fame. Even with their glaring faults, the likes of Abraham, Isaac, Jacob, Moses (he had his faults as well), even Barak and Jephthah from the period of the Judges are listed.

It is comforting to see that God's sovereign sway is undeterred, amidst scandals and depravity. Even with leaders and followers with glaring errors, depravity, and sin, God over-rules and works all things together, including his plan to bring the Messiah from this line of scoundrels. Noting such is intended to lead us to greater praise.

Appendix A: Genesis in the Gospels (and Acts)

1.	Genealogies	Mt. 1:1-3; Luke 3:33-37	Gen. 5 & 11
2.	Abraham:	Mt. 3:9; 8:11; Mk. 12:26	
3.	Mt. 2:6	cf. with Gen. 49:10-11	
4.	Mt 5:18	with Genesis 8:22 seasons will "never cease."	
5.	Mt 11:23	Sodom (Gen. 18-19)	
6.	Mt. 19:4-5	Marriage in the beginning (Gen 1:27; 2:24)	
7.	Mark 2:27	The Sabbath (often), the 7th day of creation	
8.	Mark 10:6-9	Origin of Marriage	
9.	Mark 12:26-27	The God of A, I, and J. also Mt. 22:32, Lk 20:37	
10.	Mark 13:19	When God created the world	
11.	Luke 1:51b (55)	Gen. 11:8; 17:7	
12.	Luke 1:72-74	Gen. 17:5; 22:16-18	
13.	Luke 13:16, 28		
14.	Luke 15:20	Gen. 33:4; 45:14-15; 46:29	
15.	Luke 16:23-3	Abraham in the afterlife	
16.	Luke 17:26-29	Noah (Gen. 6:5-8), Lot (Gen 19)	
17.	Luke 19:9	Zacchaeus, upon conversion, a child of Abraham	
18.	Luke 19:33-35	Palm Sunday colt fulfills Gen. 49:10-11	
19.	John 1:1, 10	Creation echoes (Gen. 1)	
20.	John 1:51	Jacob's Ladder (Gen. 28:12)	
21.	John 8:33-41,52-58	Before Abraham was, I am	
22.	John 8:44	Satan, a murderer from the beginning	
23.	John 16:21	Pain @ childbirth (Gen. 3:16)	
24.	John 17:5, 24	Before the world began	
25.	Acts 3:13	The God of A, I, and J	
26.	Acts 3:15	Author of life (Gen. 1)	
27.	Acts 3:25	Covenant and Abraham (Gen. 22:18)	
28.	Acts 4:24	Creator (Gen. 1)	
29.	Acts 17:24	"	
30.	Acts 7:2-19	Stephen's summary Gen. 12, 15, 37, 39, 43-45	
31.	Acts 17:26	Gen. 5	

Gen. 3:15 is a "far-reaching announcement of the long conflict between good and evil. . . . It may be said that all other prophecies of the Christ and the Kingdom of God are comprehended in the protoevangelium as in a germ." (J. Barton Payne's *Encyclopedia of Biblical Prophecy*, 311)

Appendix B: Genesis According to the Apostles

1.	Romans 2:25-29	Gen. 17
2.	Romans 4:3, 9-25	Gen. 15:6, 17:5, etc
3.	Romans 5:12-19	Gen. 2:17; Adam and Christ 1 Cor. 15:45
4.	Romans 9:6-13	Gen. 21:12; 18:10,14; Gen. 25:23
5.	Romans 11:1	Gen. 49:27
6.	Romans 16:20	Gen. 3:15-16
7.	1 Cor. 6:16	Gen. 2:24
8.	1 Cor. 15:39	Gen. 1:11, 12, 21, 24-26 'according to its kind'
9.	1 Cor 15:45	Gen. 2:7
10.	2 Cor. 4:6	Gen. 1:3
11.	Gal. 3:6-9	Gen. 15:6; 12:3; 18:18; 22:18
12.	Gal. 3:14	Gen. 16:4-5, 16 ff
13.	Gal. 3:16, 18	Gen. 12:7; 13:15; 24:7
14.	Gal. 4:21-31	Gen. 21:9-10
15.	Eph. 1:4	Gen. 1:1
16.	Eph. 5:31-32	Gen. 2:24
17.	Phil. 3:5	Gen. 49:27
18.	Col. 1:16-17	Christ, the Creator
19.	Col. 2:11-12	Gen. 17:1-4
20.	1 Tim. 2:13-14	Gen. 2:21-22; 3:1-7
21.	2 Tim. 1:9	Gen. 1 "the beginning of time"
22.	Heb. 2:16	Gen. 17:7
23.	Heb. 4:3b-4	Gen. 2:1-3
24.	Heb. 6:13-14	Gen. 22:17
25.	Heb. 7:6-7, 13-14 (5:6)	Gen. 14:18 ff
26.	Heb. 9:15-16	Gen. 15:17-18
27.	*Heb. 11:1-22*	*Gen. 1-50*
28.	Heb. 13:20a	Gen. 17:5-6
29.	James 1:15	Gen. 3:6
30.	James 2:21,23	Gen. 15:6
31.	1 Pet. 1:20	Gen. 1:1
32.	1 Pet. 3:6, 20-21	Gen. 7:23, 8:1-4
33.	2 Pet. 2:5-7	Gen. 6 and 19
34.	2 Pet. 3:5	Gen. 1
35.	Jude 7	Gen. 19
36.	Jude 11	Gen. 4
37.	Jude 14	Gen. 5:18 ff
38.	Rev. 2:7; 22:14	Gen. 2:9; 3:22
39.	Rev. 7:5-8; 21:12	Gen. 49
40.	Rev. 12:5, 9	Gen. 49:8-12; Gen. 3:15c; Jn 12:31
41.	Rev. 13:8; 17:8; 20:15	Gen. 1:1 From "the creation of the world"
42.	Rev. 21:23-25; 22:5	Gen. 1:14-19
43.	Rev. 22:2, 19	Gen 2:8-11

Made in the USA
Columbia, SC
06 November 2022